MW01243319

 VALUABLE READER BONUS!

Want insider information to shortcut the time it takes to get things done, done right, and done on time with Medicare?

As my complimentary, no cost, courtesy bonus, I'd like to gift you my "Prepare For Medicare Pre-Planning Pack" formerly reserved exclusively for my private clients who choose to go through my free Medicare SmartStart Program.

Your "Prepare For Medicare Pre-Planning Pack" gives you instant access to critical checklists and time-saving tips they don't tell you, or want you to know, <u>PLUS,</u> a first-look at the controversial chapter *You Are At War (But A War That You Can Win),* from my companion book *Shopping Medicare Smartly.* It exposes the orchestrated and organized efforts by the big insurance companies use of persuasion propaganda and how you can guard against their attack on your attention.

GET YOUR VALUABLE BONUS HERE:

StartingMedicareSmartly.com/Bonus

ALSO BY ANDREW L HIBBARD

I Love America (Co-authored with Mike Capuzzi)

The Ultimate Guide to Getting Ready for Medicare in WNY

The Ultimate Guide to Getting Started with Medicare in WNY

The Ultimate Guide to Getting Covered by Medicare in WNY

ANTICIPATED NEW RELEASES

Shopping Medicare Smartly

Escape From The Medicare Maze

STARTING MEDICARE SMARTLY

Smarter, Time-Saving Steps Proven To Help You Sign Up Stress-Free And Absolutely Avoid A Costly Late Penalty At 65 Or Anytime After

ANDREW L HIBBARD

PUBLISHED BY MEDICARE MANAGEMENT OF WNY

PROUDLY PRINTED IN THE UNITED STATES OF AMERICA

First Edition Printed March 2023

ISBN: 9798388233691

DISCLAIMER:

While all attempts have been made to verify information provided in this publication, neither the author nor the publisher assumes any responsibility for errors, omissions, or contradictory interpretation of the subject matter herein. This publication is designed to provide accurate and authoritative information with regards to the subject matter covered. However, it is sold with the understanding that the author and the publisher are not engaged in rendering legal, accounting, or other professional advice. If professional advice or other expert assistance is required, the services of a competent professional should be sought. The purchaser or reader of this publication assumes responsibility for the use of these materials and information. Adherence to all applicable laws and regulations, including federal, state and local, governing professional licensing, business practices, advertising and any other aspects of doing business is the sole responsibility of the purchaser or reader.

Dedicated to the residents of WNY who find Medicare unnecessarily confusing and complicated.

The smartest people always find a way to make complicated things...uncomplicated.

I hope *Starting Medicare Smartly* can do that for you.

If You Can Answer <u>YES</u> To These Five Questions, My "Medicare SmartStart Program" May Be Able To Help You.

1. Do you live in one of eight WNY counties? (Niagara, Erie, Chautauqua, Cattaraugus, Wyoming, Genesee, Orleans, Allegany)
2. Will you be turning 65 in the next 4-6 months?
3. Do you find the thought of dealing with Medicare directly overwhelming and frustrating?
4. Would you prefer to have someone else fill out and file all the required Medicare paperwork for you, so you don't have to spend your time or energy doing it by yourself?
5. Would you be interested in relying on a software system to instantly sort through the sea of insurance companies and accurately compare costs between each plan (over 201+) to reliably research, review and recommend where you can get the with the very best benefits, at the very best rate, the very first time you sign up?

If you can answer <u>YES</u> to these five questions, give me a call at **716-833-0252**

IMPORTANT NOTICE

Before taking any action,
please review all information provided.

The recommendations, answers, and solutions disclosed in
this book are based on the most common concerns and the
proven solutions from more than 850+ participants who have
successfully signed up and started with Medicare using my
nationally recognized Medicare SmartStart Program.

I encourage and strongly urge all readers to
double-check critical information before making
any final Medicare enrollment decisions.

Any final Medicare coverage decision remains the
obligation of each individual reader, after carefully
considering the information provided to them by
verbal, written, or other means.

CONTENTS

Part 1 – Welcome

Important! Read This First...15

Who Should Read This Book...21

Why Should You Listen To Me......................................27

My Promise To You..31

Introduction 35

Will You Start Medicare Smartly?..................................41

Part 2 – The Truth About Medicare

Myths You May Have Heard..51

What You Should Expect...55

Part 3 – Making Your Medicare Decision

Sign Up Or Suspend (You Can't Do Nothing).................67

Turning 65, Retiring, Know You Need Medicare.............71

SmartStart Story: "Late Filling Larry".................75

Turning 65, Will Keep Working, Maybe Medicare.........77

SmartStart Story: "Kept Paying Karen"..............84

Older Than 65, Retiring, Know You Need Medicare.......91

SmartStart Story: "No Proof Paul".....................96

Filling Out And Filing Your Forms................................99

Part 4 – Now What?

Why Most People Struggle, But You Won't 109

Two Choices, But Only One Makes Sense......................113

The Next Step...119

Part 5 – Appendix

Only Some Support Local Small Business, Will You?...127

Resources...138

About Andrew L Hibbard......………………………............139

About Medicare SmartStart Program..............................141

What People Are Saying..143

WNY Heroes, Inc..153

A Small Request..155

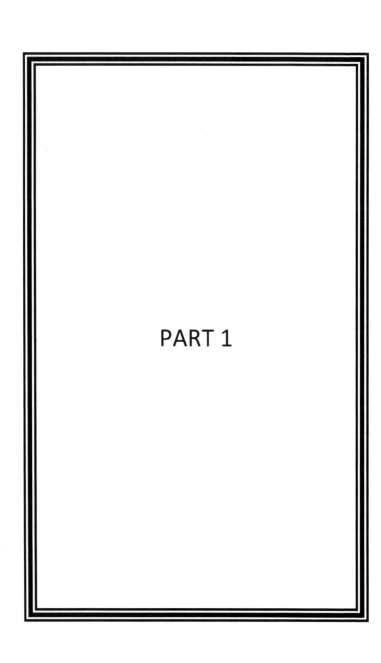

PART 1

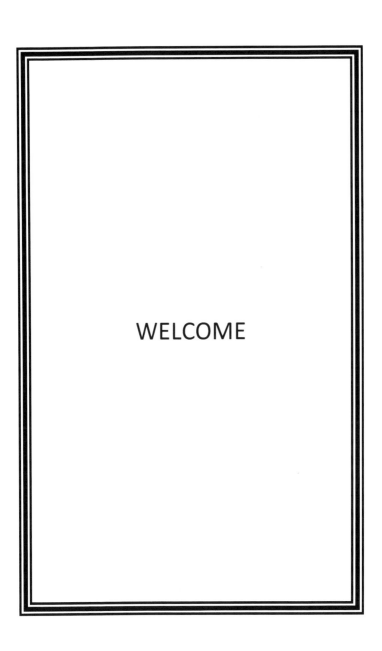

WELCOME

IMPORTANT!
READ THIS FIRST

Reader beware. The helpful Medicare services offered to you through my company, Medicare Management of WNY, is noticeably and notably different. We are known as the "anti-insurance agency" and don't act like "salespeople."

We are *Starting Medicare Specialists*, and we have made a concerted and controlled effort to offer incredibly helpful educational information first and foremost, free from any Insurance Company influence or conflict of interest.

We are not like the other "mass market" Medicare insurance mills you hear about on the local radio stations, read about in the local papers, or see on local morning television shows, all trying to convince any breathing body to talk with them about "more choices" as their stealth way to just sell you something.

You'll find comfort knowing we don't rely on a big, bloated advertising budget to tell the public what we do. We don't accept bonuses or bribes by the Insurance Companies, and we don't allow ourselves to be bullied or bought off. No "pay-to-play" for us. We don't want to. We don't need to. We don't even advertise our services --- and that is on purpose.

We are a service-based company, <u>NOT</u> a sales-based company. While others start by saying "*here's why you should buy our insurance,*" we do the opposite. We are the only Medicare experience you'll find in WNY (and the entire state of NY to our knowledge), who offer this kind of honest, unbiased, and education-first expertise.

You can feel free to take advantage of our complimentary informative reading resources --- all uniquely written for anyone pre-65 wondering what they have to do with Medicare. Or, you can rely on our one-of-a-kind, on-site Medicare concierge for helping you one-on-one, in-person, with plotting and planning when the smartest time is for you to start Medicare (or suspending Medicare until after 65).

And, when the time is right, we even have special access to submission support services to speed up and shorten the time it takes to fill out and file your application forms Medicare requires, so you won't wait the typical 90-day delay if you do-it-yourself, like everyone else who doesn't know any better.

Since 2015, my wife, Lyndsey, and I have helped more than 850+ Western New Yorkers, nearing age 65, just like you, successfully sign up and start with Medicare with our free Medicare SmartStart Program --- now, widely considered and

16

proven to be the most popular and preferred way to enjoy everything with Medicare done-for-you.

Each month, we accept a limited number of new Medicare SmartStart Program participants from the hundreds of people who ask to meet and work with us. Everything we do is by appointment only, no walk-ins. That means we can be better prepared for you and your needs, and that means it is a better use of your time. No interruptions. No distractions. Fewer clients means more time and attention on you, and we believe better results overall.

Most of our Medicare SmartStart Program participants are referred by current satisfied clients, or by the community outreach relationships we have built over the years.

In rarer cases, we may personally invite someone to meet with us. Folks who stand out as special because they are "doers," and are proactive in getting things done and things done right.

These are folks who may have requested a free copy of any, or all, of my books or asked me to send them one of my Consumer Report Guides. **If that is you, know that you are on my invitation list, and I will reach out to you personally.**

Sometimes the best advice you can get when you are nearing 65, and wondering what you need to do about Medicare, is that you do not need to sign up at all. Yes, in some situations, that is true if you plan to keep working past 65 (despite all the rumors saying otherwise), and I will tell you. I'll also tell you if you're better off doing everything on your own --- without our help.

But, if your situation passes my test, and you choose to put my free Medicare SmartStart Program to work for you, rest assured that you will receive unparalleled personal attention.

We will work on your behalf aggressively, keep you up to date on progress points, and continue constant communication step-by-step with pre-scheduled checkpoints. In fact, we will do all the dirty work dealing with Medicare directly, so you don't have to do much of anything.

We will explain the entire Medicare process to you before you need to decide on anything. Working together, we will determine how to make your move to Medicare simpler, easier, seemingly stress-free, and almost effortless.

Dedicated To Helping You Start Medicare Smartly,

ANDREW

Andrew "Mr. Medicare" Hibbard

P.S. You DO NOT need to read this entire book to connect with me and learn more about my free Medicare SmartStart Program. If interested, you can immediately take advantage of the invitation on the next page.

THE BETTER, SMARTER WAY TO SIGN UP FOR MEDICARE IN WNY YOU'VE NEVER HEARD OF!

Most folks in WNY aren't sure where to start with Medicare. And feeling forced to figure out all the fine print with what you have to do on your own is no place to be.

I have a proven, sure-fire solution for those who don't have the time or desire to deal with Medicare directly that makes the entire process, step-by-step from start to finish, simpler, easier, seemingly stress-free and almost effortless.

If you'd like to learn more about why my free Medicare SmartStart Program has quickly become the most popular and preferred way to sign up and start Medicare in WNY, and how it can be put to work for you, please request your FREE **"Medicare SmartStarter Info Kit"** today.

GET YOUR FREE INFO KIT HERE:

MedicareSmartStartWNY.com/Info

Or Call **716-833-0252** Or Scan

No Cost - No Risk - No Annoying Salesperson Will Answer

**SmartStart
Task Timer**

** Andrew's Advice: Reading the rest of Part I and Part II sequentially, in one sitting would be best.

So, grab your favorite drink, maybe a small snack bowl, and get ready to dive in --- time to rock & roll.

Also, having a pen and pad of paper may come in handy for notes.

To read these two (2) sections should take about **20-30 minutes**

WHO SHOULD READ
THIS BOOK?

As an active adult living in WNY, and nearing age 65, I'm sure you would agree it's hard enough to find time to enjoy the things you want to be doing, let alone find the time to deal with things you don't want to be doing...like anything remotely related to Medicare, right?

That's why I have written this simple and straightforward, step-by-step guidebook for people like yourself who are always on the run and in need of a smart solution to cut through all the clutter. It contains essential information to help you make a better, more informed Medicare decision.

And while I wrote *Starting Medicare Smartly* as an intentionally short book, to be read in about an hour, I want to ensure that your valuable time is well spent. You should be happy to hear all the fluff and filler has been removed. Everything specially edited down to be just a little over 100 pages so you can read in a single sitting.

My hope is to give you easily digestible instructions as quickly and effectively as possible which are relevant to you turning 65 soon so you can be best prepared and take the "scare" out of Medicare.

So, before you thumb through, please take a few minutes to read the next page or two to discover if this book is a smart investment of your time, energy, and focus.

Here's what you need to know...

As an author and sought-after Medicare speaker, I am invited to talk about all things Medicare all the time, all around the WNY area. On-site seminars. "Lunch & Learn" employee events. Interviews with WECK Radio *Senior Matters*. Articles for *Forever* Young magazine. You might be surprised at how much there actually is to talk about with Medicare.

Typically, many, if not most, of these talks are for HR Reps at small and medium size companies (less than 100 employees), who don't offer their retirees a health insurance plan paid for, or sponsored by, the company. The retiree, which might be you, has to sign up for Medicare and pick their own private insurance plan.

These HR Reps feel overwhelmed and underprepared to have "the Medicare talk" with their employees who are nearing age 65, and so the cycle continues with more and more retirees having to fend for themselves.

There is a trend whenever I speak, where someone inevitably

asks me: "Is there a way to make the whole Medicare process easier for us to understand and guide our retirees?"

Finally, through a coordinated and cooperative effort, I designed and developed the Medicare SmartStart Program to solve that problem. Feedback from the last 850+ program participants, was used to write this book you now hold in your hands.

Now, before I explain who will benefit most from reading this book, I need to make you aware of who WILL NOT benefit from reading this book. Please ask yourself these quick questions…

- Do you live outside the eight counties of WNY?
- Do you have a modified adjusted gross income below $30,000?
- Are you looking to qualify and apply for NYS Medicaid or other welfare programs?
- Are you a Federal, State, County, or Local Government retiree who will be given tax-payer funded Health Insurance in retirement managed through OPM, NYSHIP, etc?
- Did you retire from a large group employer (100 or more) and will be given retiree Health Insurance managed by a third-party benefits administrator, like, a Local Union, AON, VIA Benefits, etc?
- Do you stubbornly prefer to do things yourself even if there is free help available to make things simpler and

easier?

- Do you tend to follow the crowd and do things others do despite a lesser-known proven path to success might exist?

- Do you feel anything that mentions Medicare must be another advertisement, scam, or solicitation just trying to sell you something which makes you lack trust in it?

If so, I'm not quite sure the information inside this book will really be much value to you. You have my permission to stop reading and use your time for something else.

And if you're still here, great! Now we can really get focused on who UNDERLINE WILL benefit most from reading this book.

Starting Medicare Smartly is a guidebook specifically for you, if you are nearing age 65 (6-12 months away), and you are consciously concerned about not messing up or making any kind of mistake, major or minor, with Medicare.

You do not want to be like the majority of people who just conform to the way others do things thinking it must be a proven path to success. Others who accept Medicare is confusing and that's the way it is. That Medicare is difficult to understand, and you must struggle to figure it out on your own like others have done and continue to do.

You are looking for a way to make a confusing and challenging chore easier and know that "just doing the same thing others do about Medicare doesn't make it smart --- it only makes it common."

You willingly want and wish for qualified help and a bit of handholding, and see yourself as:

- You wonder what you should be doing to get ready for Medicare, and aren't sure where to start...

- You prefer to rely on in-person help from a real human, who can be held accountable, rather than dial 1-800-Numbers and talk to phone robots and play the "phone-tag tango" game...

- You feel you have worked hard, played by the rules, and over the years paid your fair share into the Medicare system --- and now want to understand what you get for all that money they've taken...

- You understand that taking a proactive role in your Medicare planning gives you the best possible outcomes and reduces all potential problems...

Lastly, and maybe important of all...

- You are a highly responsible individual who wants to shortcut all the common hurdles, hassles, and horsing around.

If you believe that sounds like you, you'll be happy to know I wrote this book just for you. The successful strategies shared will help you better prepare and get ready for Medicare so you can feel more confident you start Medicare smartly.

So, if that seems worthwhile to you, and you're ready, please keep reading...

Some people want "official" help specifically from the government or an insurance company directly thinking it's the safe and smart way to go.

SmartStart
Smart Tip

Their assistance and so-called advice is without a doubt blatantly biased to their direct benefit...not yours.

"The nine most terrifying words in the English language are 'I'm from the government and I'm here to help.' "
Ronald Reagan

WHY SHOULD YOU
LISTEN TO ME?

You may be asking yourself, *"How can you be qualified to help me with Medicare if you aren't the Federal Government and you don't work for a Medicare insurance company?"* (I get this question a lot).

Well, let me explain...

If I'm being honest, my fifth-grade career worksheet definitely did not say "talk about Medicare Insurance" when I grow up. I actually wanted to be a firefighter like my grandpa. You may like to know, I was able to accomplish this goal, spanning almost a decade with my local Volunteer Fire Department in Eggertsville, NY along with an overlapping 10-year career enlisted with the U.S. Air Force Fire Department Crash-Rescue Unit at the Reserve Base in Niagara Falls.

But, along the way, I accidentally fell face-first into the "Medicare Maze" after a tragic circumstance with my own family occurred. We were faced with an immediate concern about how to pay for the high cost of cancer treatment and associated copays that popular Medicare insurance plans around town, aren't willing and won't cover.

The subsequent financial burden brought me to work for, at the time, one of the largest Medicare Health Insurance Companies nationwide (on the Fortune 100 list and you would know if mentioned by name).

So, you see, for my family, I HAD to become a Medicare expert out of circumstance...not by choice.

Now, there are a lot of background details I am going to skip over which are only significant to me and will be insignificant to you. I'll share more with you on how I became a local Medicare advocate, professionally published Medicare author, and sought-after guest speaker on Medicare later on. What's important for you to know right now is simply the sad fact that most people stress and struggle how to get started with Medicare because they are left to fend for themselves with how to fill out and file their forms...and IT'S NOT YOUR FAULT!

Just know that the problem isn't with you...it's with the limited information you have and the lack of reliable Medicare resources available.

But here's the thing about my story...it's not really about "what" I did...it's about WHY I did it.

Can you think of anyone you know who has said dealing with Medicare was simple, easy, or straightforward? I doubt you can.

Why is that?

Everyone these days is being forced to spend their own time and energy to figure out the fine print of Medicare. The Federal Government continues to re-write the rules and regulations around Medicare enrollment, making it harder and harder to understand, while simultaneously limiting available resources adequate in providing the public accessible assistance.

You are expected to fill out and file the proper forms, at the proper time, the proper way, without any instructions, and must accept your own assumptions and hit-or-miss guesses as the only way to do things…and that's not fair!

There had to be a better way.

That's why I created my free Medicare SmartStart Program and am writing this book now. To provide a privately-funded solution to the problem the Federal Government won't solve and the Insurance companies can't.

My free Medicare SmartStart Program is the first Medicare experience in WNY of its kind where you can enjoy everything with Medicare done for you…from signing up for Part A & B…and beyond.

I hope the important information I share with you in this book will complement the important in-person assistance services my free Medicare SmartStart Program offers.

It's the success stories from the past 850+ program participants that feed my continued crusade to do what I do.

And I do all I can to make the Medicare process smooth, seamless, a bit simpler, and hopefully stress-free --- so you don't have to invest hours/days/weeks of your scarce free time sitting at home alone, in isolation, wondering if you are doing things right or messing things up and have to do it all twice...or worse, buying a costly COBRA plan because your filing date is wrong or filing late and having to pay an expensive penalty for life.

Okay, well now that you know a little about me, let's get into what I can promise you with the contents of this book...

SmartStart
Smart Tip

How many times in your life have you had an experience where you needed to learn how to do something yourself not by choice, but by circumstance?

Sometimes the best solutions to complex problems are simple --- and often not the normal way of doing things.

MY PROMISE TO YOU

I promise to make this book a valuable use of your time and attention. Within the next hour or so (hopefully less), I will open your eyes to what you need to do with Medicare for three (3) very specific situations:

- You are turning 65, and retiring, and know you need Medicare,
- You are turning 65, will continue to keep working, and you're not sure what you need to do with Medicare,
- Or you are older than 65, now retiring, and need to sign up for Medicare late, and want to avoid a lifetime late penalty.

There's a long list of things you must do to set up your Medicare benefits correctly. As you begin putting your "to-do" list together, it's tougher and tougher for WNY residents to attempt getting signed up and started with Medicare on their own, only to be misled, misinformed, or misguided --- oftentimes unknowingly. And if you're caught committing a mistake with Medicare, it can be costly, and many times it cannot be corrected once made.

That's why many readers believe this book will be a clear and concise do-it-yourself guide. You may be thinking the same way, but it is not.

In fact, feeling forced like you have to try and figure out all the fine print with Medicare is the #1 source of stress, fear, and frustration for those nearing age 65.

While the intention of this book did begin as a DIY guide, I've realized that may not be the best way to free you from those feelings of stress, fear, and frustration.

The way I see it, the last thing that would be considered helpful is asking you to do any of this yourself.

Instead, I hope this short, helpful book will show you a better, SMARTER way to get things done, and done right...WITHOUT the hassle of doing it yourself and WITHOUT having to spend a dime or much time (and likely, enjoy having it all done for you!)

But before we move on, I have a reminder for you, so please take careful note...

Regardless of the career you've had, the money you've made, or the lifestyle you live, be aware that your retirement situation and subsequent Medicare needs are unique to you, and not like anyone else's.

Very much like unique fingerprints from person to person, you have a different birthday, a different retirement date, a different day you need to submit your Medicare paperwork, a different day you need your Medicare benefits to start, you have different doctors, different prescriptions, different priorities, and personal preferences, so what worked for your friends, family, neighbors, or coworkers will likely <u>NOT</u> be what works for you --- let alone what works best for you.

If all you take away from this book is that you shouldn't attempt trying to tackle Medicare on your own, without qualified advice, I'll be happy.

You don't have to ask me for help, but certainly don't try to do everything with Medicare all yourself --- it's just not worth the risk!

SmartStart
Smart Tip

Often, more information is not actually more helpful to you.

In most cases, you don't really need more information...you just need <u>better</u> information.

Of course, I'd be remiss if I didn't mention, but if you do want more help from me than what I can offer in this short, helpful book, you can learn more about my Medicare SmartStart Program by requesting your free "Medicare SmartStarter Info Kit" below, or in the back of this book.

It's a great little overview. I'll happily put it together and send it to you at my expense --- no questions asked.

Your Medicare SmartStarter Info Kit includes an in-depth overview of the complete 3-step program (from (1) initial strategy session, to (2) secure sign up and submission session, to (3) final shopping session), PLUS, gives you a glimpse of the top things the past 850+ participants can't stop talking about, and the unfair advantage they were given relying on my proven program, like:

- The **confidence** they felt knowing things were being done for them, done right, and done on time…
- The **convenience** of everything required available in one place, and at one time…
- The **consistency** of working with the same person throughout the entire process without having to keep starting over with strangers.

Request your free Medicare SmartStarter Info Kit today, and it'll be in the mail tomorrow. It's that easy.

MedicareSmartStartWNY.com/Info

INTRODUCTION

More information about Medicare? "Medicare Help," if there can be such a term, has long been disguised in trojan horse-like fashion, from out-of-state scammers, selfish salespeople, and nowadays endless TV endorsements by celebrities paid off by the insurance companies convincing you to call them for "help."

But how you define "help" is very important. It will directly determine the credibility of the information you choose to get and gather during the year before you turn 65.

This is what Merriam-Webster has to say about help...

HELP \help\ *vb* **1**: aid, assist **2**: improve, relive **3**: to be of use **4**: to change for the better **5**: to serve

I agree with the obvious descriptions of (1) aid, assist; (2)

improve, relive; or (3) to be of use, but it's the last two that really get me thinking. Really, any and all Medicare information is being advertised to aid and assist you. To supposedly relieve your stress or struggle in some way.

But I would question the integrity behind most of the information you are being offered and challenge if it meets the definition of (4) change YOU for the better, or (5) serves YOU in some meaningful way.

In fact, I would say it should be considered biased to benefit the very person putting it out. Much of it is tricking you to trust the selfish salesperson who is just trying to sell you something.

The brochures, benefit books, postcards, and pamphlets they send are to persuade and pressure you, absent of actual advice.

When I started Medicare Management of WNY and began writing books and offering educational services back around 2015, it was a combative response to the entire collection of insurances companies, their bonused, bribed and bought-off broker network, and the real lack of reliable resources available to the public.

I set out to be a fact-based, experienced-based, truth-teller, at the cost of being unsupported by the insurance companies because of my unwillingness to compromise my convictions. To remain independent and not align myself with their aggressive and alarming agendas.

The books I have written, and continue to write, along with the educational services I offer (which have matured into my nationally recognized Medicare SmartStart Program), are hands down the chosen choice for all Medicare answers, specifically by Baby Boomers in Buffalo born after 1956. All these things I do, are also --- for reasons that will soon become obvious to you --- hated and hunted down by the insurance conglomerates and those they collude with throughout our WNY community.

But I am not interested in being influenced by their interests. I am only interested in serving the interests of "my people," who I see in two groups.

One, the clear and confident baby boomer who knows what they need to do with Medicare and when to do it, and because of this known time-consuming chore, they willingly want someone else to do all the dirty work for them.

Two, the confused and concerned baby boomer who doesn't have the knowledge or know-how, not even knowing where to start with Medicare and doesn't have the time or desire to deal with any of it.

So, I wrote this book because, if you are like most people I work with, this is the first time you have had to deal with Medicare. You have questions. And as you start your search for somewhere, or someone, who can give you qualified answers and advice, you may find that most Medicare advertising doesn't actually give you any useful information about *how to understand your Medicare benefits,* or really *how to sign up and get started with Medicare.*

The ads you see say something about "be clear on your options," or "more companies, more choices," or "get more benefits," but then you realize that ALL Medicare sales agents, Medicare insurance agencies, and Medicare insurance company advertisements say something like that.

You should see that Medicare ads showing smiling senior couples skipping down the beach, or baby boomers riding bikes are all 100% meaningless when you aren't even sure what the first step is to get started with Medicare.

When it seems like all the mass Medicare marketing makes the whole process so hard to understand, all while wasting a whole lot of time, which I know is important to you...this kind of thing is all too common and makes making a wise decision about who to go to for help more important than ever.

Tell me, does this sound familiar...

You come from work after a stress-filled, busy, hectic, tough, tiring, energy-sapping battle every day, only to check your mail and find another armful of useless Medicare mailers to bring inside and pile on your kitchen table.

It can be information overload, right?

Well, here's what you really need to know. Typically, all the mass Medicare marketing mail comes from one of three sources...or a combination of them all.

1. Federal Government
2. Insurance Companies
3. Marketing Organizations

You need to be aware that these three sources, rarely, if ever, provide you with the information that actually helps to answer any of the questions you have about Medicare!

You see, these three sources only send you information that is in support of *their* goals, which are drastically different than what *your* goals are.

The Government's goal is to let you know you are eligible to sign up for your entitled Medicare Benefits --- but they don't really explain what your benefits are or how to go about activating them.

Meanwhile, the goal of all the Insurance Companies is to sell you a plan from their portfolio so they can make money.

And the goal of any third-party Marketing Organization is to generate "leads," by any means necessary, for the Insurance Companies that are paying them to do so.

But I believe your goal is drastically different. I believe your goal is to make sense of it all, right?

To actually understand WHAT Medicare benefits you are entitled to and will receive, IF it makes sense to apply for those benefits, and WHEN to do so. Maybe most importantly is HOW to do it correctly and without errors.

So, you must seek out clear, correct, complete, and credible advice that gives you all the facts and all your options without incentive or conflict of interest.

Certainly not the type of advice the Government, an Insurance Company, or a slick, scammy, Marketing

Organization can provide.

This book is meant to be a "permission slip" of sorts. In hundreds of Medicare SmartStart Strategy Sessions and ongoing decade-long relationships with personal private clients, I often find the people and personalities that benefit most from my resources and services are the ones who essentially know they want to rescind themselves of the responsibility of managing their Medicare. They seek a way to avoid spending countless hours spinning their wheels.

My end goal of this book is granting you, the reader, permission to pause, realize you are not alone, and you do not have to feel forced to figure everything with Medicare out by yourself. I am here to happily help you in any way I can.

And I will say, if you are the right reader, the feedback here from the previous Medicare SmartStart Program participants will "ring true" to answer all of your questions as you near age 65, and you will think: *"FINALLY! Someone really understands what I am asking and is explaining what I need to be doing in a simple and easy-to-understand way. FINALLY, someone is giving me the straight scoop."*

You may find that some of your Medicare questions still need answering, and that's okay. You may also find some things here hard to swallow or, certainly contrary to everything you may have heard or assumed (like you must sign up at 65 or you get a penalty). The advice I share with you may be quite eye-opening if you force yourself to consider it carefully.

WILL YOU START
MEDICARE SMARTLY?

There are obvious trends and traits one can observe to recognize and recall successful patterns and practices in particular populations of people. The very basis for the important information I have shared with you in this eye-opening book was, in fact, from an organized and orchestrated poll where I surveyed and solicited advice from the last 850+ pre-65 Western New Yorkers who participated in my Medicare SmartStart Program.

It became outwardly obvious what the most successful of the program participants did differently. (Successful being defined as lowest stress levels, shortest amount of time for application approval, and willingness to transfer their trust in me and refer friends or family).

The proof is in the pudding they say and armed with their feedback and findings, I have creatively crafted seven of the most common characteristics and smartest Medicare strategies, into a clever acronym S.T.A.R.T.E.R., which I would encourage you to ask yourself, do you see yourself as a Medicare Smart S.T.A.R.T.E.R., and therefore, will you start Medicare smartly?

And, as I explain and expand on my S.T.A.R.T.E.R. identity definition for you in just a moment, I wholeheartedly acknowledge that no framework or formula can address the many complexities and complications between individual Medicare scenarios and situations.

There will, of course, be nuances in how these examples are applied in varying contexts and the coordination of your coverage. There is no universal guide to signing up and starting Medicare the same way, at the same time, for all people and parties involved because no two situations are the same.

That being said, I do believe that anyone who relies on and relates to what it means to be a Medicare Smart S.T.A.R.T.E.R. will see a drastically different outcome to their Medicare experience and the effort exerted than those around town who do not know what you now know.

My hope is to show you why, if you identify as a Medicare Smart S.T.A.R.T.E.R., you are the exact type of person I go out of my way to work with, and what you should know about the unfair advantages my free Medicare SmartStart Program will offer you.

See what I mean on the next page...

S tart your Medicare planning early

T ake it slow, no need to rush

A sk for qualified help, don't do it all yourself

R ely on expert advice in your local area

T alk in-person and avoid out-of-state scams

E ducation not solicitation

R emain in control of your own choices

S tart Your Medicare Planning Early – You believe that *"the early bird gets the worm."* You see that to have a simple and stress-free move to Medicare, you should start your Medicare pre-planning process minimally 6 months before turning 65. (If you are within 3-4 months of turning 65 you are at a dire disadvantage and need to call me immediately to set up a priority strategy session at 716 . 833 . 0252)

T ake It Slow, No Need To Rush – You are not a procrastinator. You do not like feeling rushed into making hasty decisions due to a time crunch last minute. You prefer to have a planned-out path that is designed and developed to hold you by the hand, step-by-step, from start to finish, so you feel confident things are done, done right, and done on time.

Ask For Qualified Help, Don't Do It All Yourself – You know sometimes learning a new skill is worth the short-term struggle for the long-term satisfaction, when there is no real financial risk involved, like learning to garden, or teaching yourself to tile. But you also know when you're in over your head and messing up your Medicare is not worth taking the risk. You want to avoid the typical DIY disaster.

Rely On Expert Advice In Your Local Area – You are annoyed at the lack of reliable Medicare resources provided to you as a hard-working, tax-paying person, soon-to-be 65. You question why they force you to figure out Medicare on your own and would appreciate freeing yourself from these frustrations and fears by relying on the luxury of a local expert's honest effort to make your challenging chore...easier.

Talk In Person And Avoid Out-Of-State Scams – You are rightfully skeptical and suspicious of relentless out-of-state scams sent to you by mail and all those pesky and persistent 1-800 call center solicitations. You prefer and prioritize an in-person conversation, face-to-face, where you hold that person accountable for their actions and advice.

Education Not Solicitation – You accept the Medicare Mass-Marketing Machine is real and there is an assault on your attention. You recognize and repel any and all advertising that is branded by insurance companies to protect yourself against their smoke-and-mirror games, gimmicks, and tricky tactics attempting to try selling you their stuff. You just want the need-to-know facts from a trustworthy, truth-telling teacher so you feel educated about your options and empowered to make a more informed decision.

Remain In Control Of Your Own Choices – While you tell yourself you just want someone to *"do this all for you,"* you do not actually want to give up responsibility over your own choices. You reject the usual predator-prey, high-pressure pursuit the mass-marketing Medicare insurance mills use that you see all over our local tv and read about in the local paper. You prefer and prioritize a casual conversation to simply share your situation with someone who can prescribe and present solutions, not show you brochures and booklets to sell you something, leaving you feeling persuaded, pushed, and pressured to pick one plan over another.

Identifying yourself as a Medicare Smart S.T.A.R.T.E.R.

will give you a great head start so you can hit the ground running in the right direction with what is needed to be done with Medicare at 65 --- or any time after 65.

In Part 2 of this book, I will raise some questions which are pretty powerful, if taken seriously. You can read through them quickly or slowly, you choose.

Come back to anything you are confused or maybe concerned about. Certainly, don't feel like you have to get and grasp everything the first go around. There is no test. And unlike school, cheating by asking for help to get correct answers is highly encouraged.

How you choose to continue will directly determine your ability to have an enjoyable, smooth, and seamless Medicare experience --- or a potentially problematic and painful move to Medicare like the rest of the public constantly complains about.

And if you're faint at heart, maybe freaking out, or already feel a little overwhelmed and worried wanting to have your hand held so you know for sure you don't mess anything up with Medicare, answer the five (5) quick questions on the next page, and see if putting my proven Medicare SmartStart Program makes sense for you.

Otherwise, if you want to move deeper down into the Medicare Maze skip to page 51 to discover some Medicare myths you may have heard of but are 100% untrue and totally false...

If You Can Answer <u>YES</u> To These Five Questions, My "Medicare SmartStart Program" May Be Able To Help You.

1. Do you live in one of eight WNY counties? (Niagara, Erie, Chautauqua, Cattaraugus, Wyoming, Genesee, Orleans, Allegany)
2. Will you be turning 65 in the next 4-6 months?
3. Do you find the thought of dealing with Medicare directly overwhelming and frustrating?
4. Would you prefer to have someone else fill out and file all the required Medicare paperwork for you, so you don't have to spend your time or energy doing it by yourself?
5. Would you be interested in relying on a software system to instantly sort through the sea of insurance companies and accurately compare costs between each plan (over 201+) to reliably research, review and recommend where you can get the with the very best benefits, at the very best rate, the very first time you sign up?

If you can answer <u>YES</u> to these five questions, give me a call at **716-833-0252**

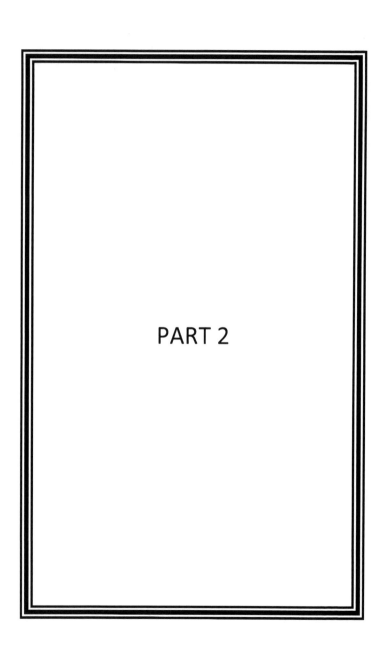

PART 2

THE TRUTH ABOUT
MEDICARE

**SmartStart
Smart Tip**

Be wary of taking advice from
anyone, or any place, that may
have a motive to their message.

All sales staff sell. Brokers broker.
And advice from your same-aged peers
is likely the blind leading the blind.

"In the land of the blind,
the one-eyed man is king."
Desiderius Erasmus

MYTHS YOU MAY HAVE HEARD

Have you heard the horror stories about Medicare from your friends, family, neighbors, or coworkers? Without knowing *exactly* what was said, I'd wager they are mostly hyperbole and elaborate embellishments or exaggerations.

It is true that dealing with Medicare directly is painfully frustrating. I think everyone would agree dialing 1-800-Numbers, to talk with phone robots and play "phone tag tango" should be avoided at all costs. This is a universal truth.

But there are, however, some myths being told around town by three (3) sources to steer clear of. They are: (1) some self-educated seniors who believe they rightfully know-it-all about Medicare even though they are wrong about most things, most of the time, (2) the hourly shift workers and sales staff at the insurance companies sales centers --- specifically those who work directly for and wear the company costume and are trained to tell you only what the company wants you to know with well-rehearsed persuasive pitches, and lastly (3) the fee-based brokers who use predatory pressure, talking in absolutes (like, "you must," or "you have to" do this or that), to manipulate your mind in a way to cause concern and confusion so you do what they want.

Here are some common myths and misrepresentations about Medicare that just aren't true, and you do not need to believe...

- When you turn 65, you have to sign up for Medicare, otherwise you will pay a late penalty

- If you want to keep working past 65, you do not have to sign up for Medicare

- You have to sign up for your Medicare benefits at the same time you sign up for your Social Security Income benefits

- You have to sign up for your Medicare benefits by going to your local Social Security office assigned to your zip code

- All people/places that advertise Medicare insurance can show you all the same companies you can compare, the same plan options you can pick, or the same prices you will pay

- All people/places that can talk to you about Medicare do the same thing, so it doesn't matter who you talk to or trust

- All people/places that can talk to you about Medicare have the same ability, authority, credibility, expertise, and experience to handle your situation start to finish

- You can sign up for Medicare Part A and Part B, but you do not need to buy a Prescription Drug plan if you do not have any medications

- Every Medicare insurance company basically offers the same kind of coverage at about the same price, so there's no need to shop around

- The advice your HR Rep gives you about what to do with Medicare, and when, it usually correct and credible

- When you sign up for Medicare, you should call the insurance company you have at work and sign up for their Medicare plan because you already have a history with them

- Once you sign up for a private Medicare insurance plan, you can only change your private Medicare insurance plan once per year

- Medigap plans are better than Medicare Advantage plans -OR- Medicare Advantage plans are better than Medigap plans

- If you want a Medicare Supplement plan, you have to buy it within 6 months of turning 65, otherwise you may not be able to get one later in life, or you will have to go through medical underwriting and will be denied

SmartStart
Smart Tip

If you take the time to learn what you need to do with Medicare so that things are done right, you won't do things wrong.

And if you don't do things wrong with Medicare, you won't have to spend the rest of your life trying to fix the things that are wrong to get things right.

WHAT YOU SHOULD EXPECT

Did you receive your 120-page *"Medicare & You" Handbook* yet? Everyone gets it, but few people read it. Out of the 40 or so Medicare SmartStart Strategy Sessions I schedule each and every month, I would say that more often than not, most folks bring their government issue handbook with them when we meet and the spine isn't even cracked.

I've even had one guy come into my hidden little office in Clarence, referred by his HR Department at MOOG. He worked as an Aerospace Engineer (literally a rocket scientist) saying *"I'm a relatively smart guy, but it takes more than a rocket scientist to figure this fine print out. I need a simple solution to this complicated problem."*

So, why all the confusion and complication with Medicare?

It seems like the "Medicare Marketing Machine" (a term I made up years ago to describe the massive, multi-million-dollar, organized effort to mislead, misinform, and misguide you) makes the whole process so hard to understand, all while wasting a whole lot of time, which I know is important to you.

This kind of thing is all too common and makes making a wise decision about who to go to for help with Medicare more important than ever.

And nearing age 65 brings about new changes you have not faced before. More than likely, while working, your health insurance was provided for you by your company, and you didn't do much work about choosing which company and coverage was best --- that's what HR did --- and like the insurance options or not, you got what you got.

Well, with Medicare, you don't get an HR Department to make your move to Medicare easier, so the whole experience can be overwhelming and certainly feel stressful.

There are four (4) frustrating factors I'd like to share with you to set the standard and explain what you should expect with Medicare, so you can be best prepared during your pre-65 planning phase.

FRUSTRATING FACTOR 1:
DANGEROUS DING DONG SALES

Think door-to-door sales is a thing of the past? Think again. There are new rules and regulations being written, and re-written, to combat the revival of this door-to-door danger to provide more protection for those potentially targeted.

This sleazy sales tactic is more common in urban areas where the population of potential prospects is more dense --- kind of like how burglars pick communities to break into.

Much like those problematic and pesky phone calls, insurance company salespeople CAN NOT SHOW UP UNANNOUNCED, you have to invite them. If you do ask a salesperson to show up, there is a lengthy process and procedure to document you're doing so.

Always be careful and cautious when an unexpected stranger shows up at your doorstep.

FRUSTRATING FACTOR 2: NON-STOP MAILBOX MARKETING

If it hasn't started already, it will. Get a bin, a box, or a bag, and set it aside to start the burn pile. You will not believe the massive amount of mail you will be sent.

I've had new clients referred to the office, and at least once weekly, bring in their collection to clarify what is critical and should be saved versus what is complete crap and can be tossed in the trash.

Here's what you need to know about those insurance company ads, and how to protect yourself from being fooled.

There are three types of marketing mail you will see shoved into your mailbox...seemingly daily. I will explain all three types first, then give a simple strategy to capture and catalog everything to save your sanity and make some sense of it all.

The first type of Medicare marketing mail is directly from the Federal Government. It usually will have the Department of Health & Human Services (DHS) logo emblazoned in the upper left corner by the return address. Sometimes, it will be official correspondence from the Centers For Medicare & Medicaid Services (CMS). Either way, this mail looks so "official" people actually assume it's a scam and accidentally throw it out --- initial issue Medicare card and all. Whoops!

It should go without saying, but official mail from the Federal Government should be kept, and kept in a safe place, and kept separate from the next two types of mail.

The second type of Medicare marketing mail can be considered sales solicitations sent directly from Insurance companies. They will be photographic postcards, benefit highlight brochures, smiling senior faces on flyers, etc. and will have the big, dumb company logo of whoever sent it all over, usually larger than your name, because they want you to remember they are more important and the ones paying the price to persistently prey upon you.

These sales solicitations will typically talk about choices the company offers, costs for the coverage, and the copays you'll pay for care. Most of it unhelpful, because each company strategically discloses only the best benefits *they* offer compared to their competitors, so no two ads put side-by-side will show you an objective comparison.

The third type of Medicare marketing mail is from third-party Marketing Organizations who are paid to generate "leads" for the insurance companies paying them. I guess Insurance Companies got smart and realized the general public was becoming skeptical and suspicious of all the sales solicitations being sent and response rates dropped. This is their covert way of catching your attention anyway.

Most Marketing Organizations' use "mass mail" and a general and generic group of names and addresses they send some sort of something to get you to respond by sending them back the enclosed business reply card, or BRC.

Typically, the headlines on these ads are cloaked in curiosity, like "Did You Know You Can Get This Benefit Based On Your Zip Code?" or "You Could Be Missing Out On These Extra Medicare Benefits!"

Most people are hip to the "bait and switch" tactics so obvious with these out-of-state scammers.

All Medicare marketing mail that is sent with the intent of a sales solicitation must be marked as such, with the following phrase: "This is a solicitation for insurance. We do not offer every plan available in your area. Any information we provide is limited to those plans we do offer in your area. For a complete list of available plans, please contact 1-800-Medicare (TTY users should call 1-877-486-2048), 24 hours a day/7 days a week, or consult www.medicare.gov"

The best way I have found for my clients is putting in place, what I call the at-home "5-Folder Scam Security Safeguard."

It's the smartest way for you to remain vigilant and protect yourself from becoming another advertising victim. To learn what it is, and how it can help you, detailed instructions are included in my free Reader Book Bonus when you access your "Prepare For Medicare Pre-Planning Pack." See Inside Cover.

FRUSTRATING FACTOR 3:
EXCESSIVE & AGGRESSIVE PHONE CALLS

You don't have to worry about these problematic and pesky phone calls until three to maybe four months before you turn 65. Once they start though, they are ongoing and obnoxious.

Much like the out-of-state scammers sending you sales solicitations by mail, I can say with clear confidence and certainty that anyone and everyone calling you by phone to talk about Medicare is a telemarketer trying to sell you something.

How do I know?

Because every year, I sit through compliance certification courses, which require multiple exams and testing procedures to be passed, reinforcing the fact that anyone working for, or representing Medicare, or the Federal Government WILL NOT and CAN NOT call you.

So, I don't think it takes Sherlock Holmes to deduce if the government ain't the one calling you about something official, it only leaves the telemarketers and the out-of-state scammers trying to get away with something.

FRUSTRATING FACTOR 4:
MESS UPS & MISUNDERSTANDINGS

The final factor I would like to share with you is regarding the mess ups and misunderstandings many, if not most folks, mistakenly make when trying to decode and decipher the difference between Medicare "Parts" and Medicare "Plans."

Let me explain…

When referring to Medicare, those in the know understand the term is in reference to the Federal Government Healthcare System. The benefits you are entitled to through Medicare only relate to Medicare Part A and Medicare Part B. Part A covering in-patient hospital services, and Part B covering outpatient medical services.

But what about Medicare Part C, or Medicare Part D?

To keep things as simple as possible for all intents and purposes with this book, Medicare Part C references Medicare Advantage Plans as an all-encompassing term, and Medicare Part D refers to Prescription Drug Plans. Of course, there are some similarities between Medicare Advantage plans, and some significant differences that, when knowing, will directly determine if you'll overpay like others, or if you'll enjoy the best value around town.

To add to the confusion, you now know of the Medicare "Parts," A, B, C, and D, plus there are also Medicare "Plans" sharing the same letters of the alphabet, and many more, going by the names of Plan A, B, C, D, F, G, L, M, N.

So, it is understandable that you may feel crazy and confused about the chaotic nature of any information you may receive about Medicare and how to make sense of it all. One letter might say "You have to do something with Medicare Part A, while the next letter might suggest you do something with Medicare Plan A. Or another letter says something about signing up for Medicare Part B, and a later letter you read tells you to buy Medicare Plan B.

While I want to over-simplify Medicare for you, so you can stop stressing and start focusing, now is not the right time or place to do so, and I will circle back on this later in the book when we dive deep into how to pick your insurance plan.

At this point, I'd like to lay out my straightforward, step-by-step plan, which will help you go from confused and concerned to calm, clear-headed and confident. It will keep YOU in control of deciding what to do with YOUR Medicare benefits and make things simpler and somewhat stress-free.

Moving forward, you will need (1) some more education around Medicare, (2) some guidance and handholding about what to do and when to do it, and eventually (3) a proven plan of attack to get you running in the right direction and on a smart path.

My intention with the rest of this book is to accomplish all three. And, while it will require you to put forth *some* effort, I believe the end results will be well worth it, and ultimately everything will become easier and almost effortless. I just ask that you trust the process. That point about trust may very well be my most important, so I will repeat for effect. I ask that you TRUST THE PROCESS.

By doing so, you'll have the chance to join the 850+ other WNY'ers who were once proactively planning as a pre-65-year-old, in the same, or similar spot you are now, and choose to trust my Medicare SmartStart Program to get things with Medicare done right, done on time, and enjoyed having it all done for them, without costing a dime.

Now, as you imagine what a luxury that would be, I'd like to move into Part 3 of the book and help you with making your Medicare decision, like if you even need Medicare at 65, or maybe not, and what you have to (or don't have to) do.

By reading through Part 3, you'll discover much more about Medicare than others ever do. And investing your time in this way will give you an undisputed unfair advantage...and who doesn't want that?

**SmartStart
Smart Tip**

Without taking a proactive role in your Medicare planning, your ability to make the best possible decision flies like a bird right out the window.

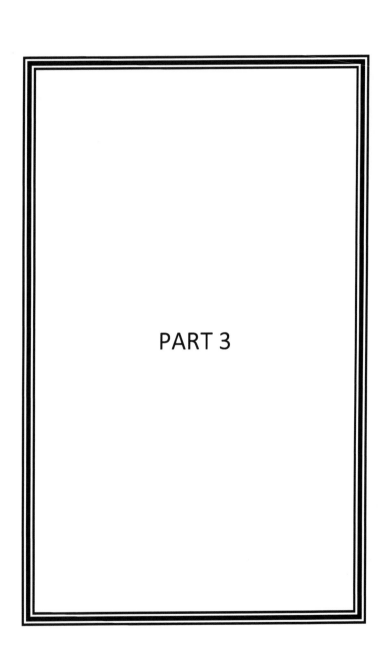

PART 3

MAKING YOUR
MEDICARE DECISION

SmartStart
Task Timer

Part III will now get into the nitty
gritty about certain situations --- not
everything will apply to you.

** Andrew's Advice: All readers
should start with "Sign Up Or
Suspend" and then select which
section they should jump to next
based on their individual needs.

In total, your specific section should
take about **10-15 minutes**

SIGN UP OR SUSPEND?
(YOU CAN'T DO NOTHING)

Today, more than ever, baby boomers in Buffalo, who were born in 1957 or later, need to seek out correct, credible, and accurate advice to help them make smart decisions about their Medicare benefits. There is just much more complexity to deciding what you should do, or have to do, about signing up and starting Medicare than in years past.

You see, before 2008, anyone turning the magic age of 65, retired, signed up and started Medicare for their health insurance, and signed up and started collecting their Social Security benefits for their supplemental income to financially support themselves in retirement all at the same time.

Since 2008, the Federal Government continues to change what they deem and determine your full-retirement age will be, kicking the can further and further down the road, increasing the eligible age older and older --- meanwhile, the Medicare eligible age has remained the same *at 65,* (unless awarded Medicare early in life due to disability).

Here is a quick-reference look at what your Federally approved, assigned and arbitrary retirement age is:

Born before 1943	Collect Social Security at age 65
Born 1943 – 1954	Collect Social Security at age 66
Born in 1955	Collect Social Security at age 66+2
Born in 1956	Collect Social Security at age 66+4
Born in 1957	Collect Social Security at age 66+6
Born in 1958	Collect Social Security at age 66+8
Born in 1959	Collect Social Security at age 66+10
Born in 1960	Collect Social Security at age 67
Born after 1960	???

And as the Federal Government continues to mismanage the largest publicly funded Ponzi scheme in history, I can only imagine that the full-retirement age will soon be 70, 75, or older (but only if they can manage to keep enough money in the account for that long).

Regardless of your full retirement age, and what you choose to do about your Social Security income benefits, you still have to wonder and worry about Medicare at 65. And quite frankly, most people wrongly assume what that can, and should, do.

Before I share with you the 'how' to do everything with Medicare, we first need to get into the 'which' move with

Medicare you need to make, and 'when' you need to do it.

There are new rules, regulations and requirements recently written into the Consolidated Appropriations Act, passed under the Biden Administration.

Similar to the Affordable Care Act passed under the Obama Administration, these new Medicare changes serve to benefit Big Pharma, and the Big Dumb Insurance Companies, while adding more confusion and challenges to you, the consumer.

My hope is not to scare you, but make you more aware, so you feel more educated and empowered.

Now, folks in WNY who work with me privately, and choose to put my free Medicare SmartStart Program to work for them, are given a custom-created ""myMedicare SmartPath" Guide Map. (You should think of your SmartPath Guide Map like a detailed explanation of the exact steps you need to take, so you know where you need to go with Medicare and when it needs to be done --- along with powerful ways to protect and preserve your financial security in retirement).

I realize though that not everyone is going to want me to hold their hand, so on the next few pages I have shared with you some preemptive and preliminary questions all participants going through my free Medicare SmartStart Program will ask and answer themselves to help reveal if it is financially favorable to sign up for Medicare at 65 --- or suspend.

The qualifying questions I share are an adequate, but abridged, version of what I use in person, and while incomplete, going through them should get you running in the right direction.

I have explained some common scenarios in an easy-to-understand way, for you to quickly read over and determine where you see yourself and your unique situation.

Based on how you answer each question, you will be led to your next step...and the next...to create the starting steps for what your move to Medicare will look like.

Think of this as an interactive reader experience, kind of like the old *Choose Your Own Adventure* book series written by Edward Packard, made popular in the 1980s, that you may remember your kids probably reading.

PRE-65 MEDICARE PLANNING PROCESS

Scenario 1: You are planning to retire at 65, and know you need Medicare...**turn to page 71**

Scenario 2: You are planning to keep working past 65, and not sure what you should do about Medicare...**turn to page 77**

POST-65 MEDICARE PLANNING PROCESS

Scenario 3: You are older than 65, now retiring, and need to sign up for Medicare late without paying the costly penalty...**turn to page 91**

QUALIFYING QUESTIONS TO SIGN UP
AND START MEDICARE AT AGE 65

(1) If you are turning 65 and plan to retire --- will you also collect your Social Security Income benefits, or delay them until a later date?

    a. If 'YES,' you will have one less step when signing up and starting Medicare at 65

    b. If 'NO,' you will have one more step when signing up and starting Medicare at 65

(2) If you are turning 65 and plan to retire --- do you have the option of retiree health insurance from your employer (an Employer Group Health Plan, or EGHP)?

    a. If 'YES,' do they require you to sign up for Medicare Part A?

    b. If 'YES,' do they require you to sign up for Medicare Part B?

    c. If 'YES,' you will be forced to pay the Medicare monthly premium, in addition to the monthly price of your retiree plan, so make sure to compare coverage and costs between keeping your retiree plan or dropping it to pick a private Medicare plan. (More times than not, Medicare makes more financial sense).

    d. If 'NO,' you HAVE TO sign up for Medicare.

(3) Does your Employer HR Department offer to fill out and file your Medicare forms, and coordinate your coverage for you? Or will you have to complete on your own?

   a. If 'YES,' do they know the new rules, regulations, and requirements to ensure you do not have the typical 90-day processing delay?

   b. If 'NO,' you will have your work cut out for you, so be sure to set aside some time to learn these new rules, regulations, and requirements.

(4) Do you know when your *Initial Enrollment Period* begins? Or when your enrollment deadline expires?

(5) Will you qualify for "Premium-free" Medicare Part A? Or will you have to pay monthly for Medicare Part A?

(6) Everybody is assessed a monthly Medicare Part B premium based on your income from the last two years (ironically, likely your highest earning years while working). Do you know how much you will pay for your monthly Medicare Part B premium?

(7) Once your Medicare Part A and Part B have been activated, will you stay "bare" with Original Medicare, or choose to buy an additional private insurance plan?

(8) If you choose to buy an additional private insurance plan, do you understand what Medicare Part A covers, Medicare Part B covers, Medicare Part C covers, Medicare Part D covers, and the drastic differences between Medicare Supplement, Medigap, and Medicare Advantage?

(9) Are you aware that there are now 11 different companies available for residents in WNY to compare and choose for private Medicare insurance (totaling over 201+) plans, each with different doctor networks, participating hospitals, preferred pharmacies and drug prices, as well as benefits beyond Medicare?

SMART STEPS TO SIGN UP AND START MEDICARE AT AGE 65

If you have found yourself here, you must be nearing age 65, planning to retire, and know you need to sign up and start Medicare. You likely have no other health insurance option in retirement other than Medicare.

This is the standard situation, similar to many of your friends and family members who worked hard, played by the rules, and scrimped, saved, and sacrificed along the way only to be slightly screwed in retirement not being rich, but not being poor. (This is anyone who did not retire from a local, State, or

Federal Government job, and provided with a free healthcare plan, paid for by us the taxpayers, given to them in retirement --- they have no need for Medicare).

Now, signing up and starting Medicare is not simple...but I will do my best to make it simpler.

The Federal Government keeps changing their rules and regulations around how they want you to fill out and file your application forms, where they need to be submitted, and when they need to be submitted by.

I spend countless hours keeping up to date on these critical changes and have done all the hard work for you. Here's what you need to know...

Clearly understanding exactly when to apply for Medicare may be the single, most important thing you need to know because not getting this right the first time can cost you thousands of dollars extra over your lifetime.

To be technical, you should not apply for Medicare at 65, rather you should apply *before* you turn 65, so that your benefits will begin exactly on the first day of the month you hit the ever important big 65th birthday.

For you folks who wish and want their Medicare benefits to begin right at age 65, you will use your specific *Initial Enrollment Period*, or in industry acronym jargon, your "IEP".

Your IEP is a 7-month period that opens in the year you turn 65, starting 3 months before your birth month, includes your birth month, and closes 3 months after your birth month. I like pictures, so hopefully this one helps...

3 Months Before Your
65ᵗʰ Birthday

3 Months After Your
65ᵗʰ Birthday

MEDICARE SMARTSTART STORY:
"LATE FILING LARRY"

To put this in perspective, we can use Larry, who was born on June 30, 1958, as an easy explained example. Larry can apply for his Medicare benefits as early as March 1st in the calendar year he will turn 65, during his birth month of June, and up until September 30th of the same calendar year.

As long as Larry fills out and files his Medicare forms between March 1st and May 31st, his Medicare coverage will begin 06/01--- the first day of his birth month, in the year he turns 65. No gap, no lapse, and no double coverage with work, or having to buy a costly COBRA plan to bridge the gap of poor planning. Smooth and seamless as expected.

However, there are several strict rules and regulations for those who dilly-dally and don't file their forms before their birthday.

While, yes, you can apply for Medicare during the three months after your birth month, you need to take note that the restrictions placed upon your application can cause you to be assessed an annoying and expensive late enrollment penalty (which you pay for life) and consequently have a delay in your coverage start date...or both --- paying a penalty and a delay.

So, if Larry did not fill out and file his Medicare forms before June 1st, he would likely be looking at paying a pricey penalty, and definitely have a delayed start date, due directly to his own delinquency. With proper planning, this can be completely avoided. Don't be like Larry who filed his forms late.

You have now learned 'which' move to make with Medicare and 'when' to make it. Your next step is to learn 'how' to fill out and file them correctly, on time, and without errors. **Turn to page 99...**

QUALIFYING QUESTIONS TO SEE *IF* YOU SHOULD SIGN UP AND START MEDICARE AT AGE 65 --- OR SUSPEND

(1) If you are turning 65 and plan to keep working --- do you work for an employer with <u>MORE THAN</u> 20 employees?

   a. If 'YES,' you <u>MAY NOT</u> need to sign up for Medicare at the present time but make sure to compare coverage and costs between keeping your work insurance plan or dropping it for a private Medicare insurance plan. (If your work plan makes more financial sense, it is imperative you pre-file your preliminary "Proof of Credible Coverage" form so you can avoid the costly lifetime late enrollment penalty later).

   b. If 'NO,' meaning you work somewhere with 19 or less employees, you <u>MAY HAVE TO</u> sign up for Medicare, even if you can keep your health insurance from your employer, so you'll need to do your due diligence and confirm.

(2) If you are turning 65, plan to keep working, and you work for an employer with <u>MORE THAN</u> 20 employees --- is your health insurance plan a high deductible plan? Terrible coverage you do not like and wish, or want, to be better? More expensive to buy than Medicare?

a. If 'YES,' you <u>MAY WANT</u> to drop your health insurance plan from your employer and sign up for Medicare and pick a private Medicare plan because the coverage, as well as cost, makes more financial sense.

b. If 'NOT SURE,' you <u>MAY WANT</u> to compare coverage and costs between keeping your work insurance plan or dropping it to sign up and start Medicare and pick a private Medicare insurance plan. (If your work plan makes more financial sense, it is imperative you pre-file your preliminary "Proof of Credible Coverage" form so you can avoid the costly lifetime late enrollment penalty later).

c. If 'NO,' meaning you love your health insurance plan from work, you <u>MAY NOT</u> need to sign up for Medicare at the present time but it is imperative you pre-file your preliminary "Proof of Credible Coverage" form so you can avoid the costly lifetime late enrollment penalty later.

(3) If you choose to suspend your Medicare at age 65, does your Employer HR Department offer to fill out and file your preliminary "Proof of Credible Coverage" form, and coordinate your coverage for you? Or will you have to complete on your own?

a. If 'YES,' do they know the new rules, regulations, and

requirements passed in the Consolidated Appropriations Act to ensure you do not have the typical 90-day processing delay?

b.   If 'NO,' you will have your work cut out for you, so be sure to set aside some time to learn these new rules, regulations, and requirements.

(4) If you are turning 65 and plan to continue working --- does your employer require you to sign up for Medicare Part A?

a.   If 'YES,' will you qualify for "premium-free" Part A? Or will you have to pay monthly for Medicare Part A?

b.   If 'NO,' it is imperative you pre-file your preliminary "Proof of Credible Coverage" form so you can avoid the costly lifetime late enrollment penalty later.

(5) If you are turning 65 and plan to continue working --- does your employer require you to sign up for Medicare Part B?

a.   If 'YES,' do you know how much you will pay for your monthly Medicare Part B premium? (Everybody is assessed a monthly Medicare Part B premium based on your income from the last two years which, ironically, is likely your highest earning years while working).

b.   If 'NO,' it is imperative you pre-file your preliminary "Proof of Credible Coverage" form so you can avoid the costly lifetime late enrollment penalty later.

(6) Is your current cost for health insurance from work (an Employer Group Health Plan, or EGHP) more expensive, or less expensive, than what it would cost for you to move to Medicare?

(7) Are there other people (spouse or dependents) who are currently insured by you carrying health insurance through your Employer, but will need to choose and buy their own coverage if you move to Medicare?

(8) Will it be more advantageous to your current family finances and future financial security to move to Medicare, and have your spouse, or dependents, or both, choose and buy their own coverage --- or for you to remain paying the current cost for health insurance from work (an Employer Group Health Plan, or EGHP)?

(9) If you choose to sign up and start Medicare at 65 and continue to work, will you stay "bare" with Original Medicare, or choose to buy an additional private insurance plan?

(10)   If you choose to buy an additional private insurance plan, do you understand what Medicare Part A covers, Medicare Part B covers, Medicare Part C covers, Medicare Part D covers, and the drastic differences between

Medicare Supplement, Medigap, and Medicare Advantage?

(11) Are you aware that there are now 11 different companies available for residents in WNY to compare and choose for private Medicare insurance (totaling over 201+) plans, each with different doctor networks, participating hospitals, preferred pharmacies and drug prices, as well as benefits beyond Medicare?

So, where do you see your situation? Does it make sense to sign up and start Medicare at 65, or suspend? Do you need more information? Do you have more questions that need answers? Or maybe you assumed too much ahead of time and now need to reconsider?

It's a lot, I get it. There are a lot of nuances in the numbers and some serious differences in decisions needed to be made between situations and scenarios.

Situation 1: If you are leaning toward choosing to keep working, but likely signing up and starting with Medicare at 65...**turn to page 82**

Situation 2: If you are leaning toward choosing to keep working, but likely suspending Medicare at 65...**turn to page 86**

SITUATION 1: KEEP WORKING, BUT SIGN UP AND START MEDICARE AT AGE 65

If you have found yourself here, you must be nearing age 65, and determined while you will continue to keep working (either by choice 'cause you love your job, or by circumstance 'cause you need the money), you will be signing up and starting Medicare.

Nowadays, after the passing of the "un"Affordable Care Act, employees have seen the increase in health insurance prices while experiencing the reduction of coverage, and instatement of high deductible plans, acting essentially like you are absent of any health insurance since you basically pay for costs completely out-of-pocket.

This is the most common situation and scenario I see with trailing-edge baby boomers in Buffalo. Make your move to Medicare at 65 so you have less conflict, concern, and coordination of things in the future, and hold out working until you reach the arbitrary "full retirement" age the Federal Government assigns you. This planning process keeps you in more control, giving you the flexibility and freedom to quietly quit whenever you want because you already have your health insurance set up outside of the company constraints.

Now, if you already read the previous section for those who have planned their rendezvous with retirement at 65, and know they need Medicare, much of this will sound repetitive, but rereading it might be good reinforcement.

Signing up and starting Medicare is not simple...but I will do my best to make it simpler. The Federal Government keeps changing their rules and regulations around how they want you to fill out and file your application forms, where they need to be submitted, and when they need to be submitted by. I spend countless hours keeping up to date on these critical changes and have done all the hard work for you. Here's what you need to know...

Clearly understanding exactly when to apply for Medicare may be the single, most important thing you need to know because not getting this right the first time can cost you thousands of dollars extra over your lifetime.

To be technical, you should not apply for Medicare at 65, rather you should apply *before* you turn 65, so that your benefits will begin exactly on the first day of the month you hit the ever important big 65th birthday.

For you folks planning to keep working, but now know you need Medicare benefits to begin right at age 65, you will use your specific *Initial Enrollment Period*, or in industry acronym jargon, your "IEP".

Your IEP is a 7-month period that opens 3 months before your birth month, in the year you turn 65, includes your birth month, and closes 3 months after your birth month. I like pictures, so hopefully the one I put on the next page helps...

3 Months Before Your
65ᵗʰ Birthday

3 Months After Your
65ᵗʰ Birthday

MEDICARE SMARTSTART STORY:
"KEPT PAYING KAREN"

To show you why it can make more financial sense to move to Medicare at 65, especially if you are choosing to keep working, let's use Karen, who works at Wegmans, as a case for clarity. Karen has confirmed with her husband, Ken, that the money management situation has taken a hit, her 401k is down, so working a few more years matters to their overall financial security and well-being.

Karen is relatively healthy, does her suggested annual screenings, and has a few generic medications that are cheap. Because Ken has his own health insurance plan, Karen chose a $1,500 deductible health insurance plan that costs her $217.00 per 2-week pay period, averaging about $434.00 each and every month.

Her HR representative, Holly, reminded Karen about her Medicare Initial Enrollment Period pre-65, and to not delay signing up otherwise she would have to pay a late penalty later. Because Karen would keep working, Holly said she would have to keep her health insurance from work.

Unfortunately, Holly had the best of intentions, but may

have been misinformed and therefore is misguiding Karen.

With Holly from HR's misleading information, Karen signed up for Medicare during her Initial Enrollment Period, and began paying the monthly Medicare Part B price, in addition to the $217.00 per 2-week pay period price for her health insurance at work unnecessarily.

In my opinion, what Karen could have done --- and should have done --- was sign up and start Medicare at 65 but drop her costly $217.00 per 2-week pay period deductible plan. She could have picked a private Medicare insurance plan (many of which are now $0/month) for her insurance coverage instead and enjoyed more robust coverage, with no medical deductible. That's right! Many private Medicare plans are available at no added cost above the monthly Medicare Part B premium price.

If Karen pays the $434.00 a month for the next year and 8 months until her "full retirement" age, that's close to $10,000 that could have been saved. Don't be like Karen who kept paying for her work insurance at the same time she signed up for Medicare.

You have now learned 'which' move to make with Medicare and 'when' to make it. Your next step is to learn 'how' to fill out and file them correctly, on time, and without errors. **Turn to page 99...**

SITUATION 2: KEEP WORKING, BUT SUSPEND MEDICARE AT AGE 65

If you have found yourself here, you must be nearing age 65, and determined while you will continue to keep working (either by choice 'cause you love your job, or by circumstance 'cause you need the money), you may find it more financially favorable to suspend Medicare and keep your Employer Group Health Plan, or EGHP.

This is the least common situation and scenario I see with baby boomers in Buffalo. Suspending your Medicare past age 65 is full of limits and limitations you need to be aware of to steer clear of any Government "gotchas." I will go through some proven steps you can take to sign up and start Medicare after 65 penalty-free.

But first, I have to ask, *"why are you considering suspending Medicare as 65?"*

I don't mean to be confrontational or challenge you on your decision, just doing my due diligence to confirm it's the right choice for you.

A common misconception is that health insurance through an Employer Group Health Plan, or EGHP, is better. I would argue that when properly set up and positioned, Medicare is almost always more financially favorable than keeping an EGHP past age 65.

Sometimes, you might have a younger spouse, or dependent

adult children (26 or younger) on your health insurance still. While moving to Medicare might make sense for you, it exposes them to having to buy high-cost health insurance offered by the "un"Affordable Care Act --- a painful experience nobody wants, like being poked in the eye with a sharp stick.

Your plan may be to wait until your younger spouse is 65, and then both make your move to Medicare at the same time. This is understandable, but there are steps you will need to take to protect yourself from paying a late penalty later.

Unless, for some reason, your employer requires you to sign up for Medicare Part A, or Medicare Part B, or both, you can, in fact, suspend your Medicare until a future date --- without paying a late enrollment penalty --- as long as you have what the Federal Government deems "credible coverage."

Credible Coverage must be received through an Employer, under *active* employment, where there are more than 20 employees. If you are receiving health insurance as a retiree, have chosen COBRA coverage, or are actively employed with less than 20 employees --- these situations and scenarios DO NOT count as credible coverage, and you HAVE TO sign up and start Medicare at 65. **Re-read page 77 and see page 82.**

For those of you who have some silly or strange oddball situation, there are of course exceptions to what I have outlined above. One might be if you work somewhere with less than 20 employees, but your health insurance is through an association where multiple small businesses joined together to be insured as one, single group, it may qualify as credible coverage, but we need to talk specifics before you assume anything.

Now, if you still suspect suspending Medicare at 65 makes the most sense, there are two (2) extremely important forms to fill out so you know with 100% certainty, and without question, you will not have to pay a late enrollment penalty when you sign up and start Medicare after 65.

(1) Request a "written notice of credible coverage" from the Insurance Company which provides you your health insurance (You will have to ask for this form from them directly. It is not from your employer)

(2) Pre-file a preliminary "proof of credible coverage" form documenting important information about your employer, and your employment. (This form is filled out by you, but I can do it for you, so you don't have to spin your wheels second-guessing anything)

When these forms are completed and verified correct, you cannot actually file them anywhere, yet. Eventually, when you do sign up and start Medicare after 65, these two forms will allow you to shortcut many of the hassles and hurdles others will horse around with and make your Medicare process much more stress-free.

If you do not have these forms filled out and pre-filed, you will need to produce and provide the following alternative proof of credible coverage in the future to possibly waive paying the late enrollment penalty:

(1) A written letter, on company letterhead, signed by a company official, including official's title, official office contact information (must include telephone number), and date.

(2) Income tax returns for each year eligible for Medicare but not enrolled, showing health insurance premiums paid.

(3) Year-end W-2s reflecting any and all pre-tax medical contributions (HSA, FSA, etc).

(4) Paystubs per pay period reflecting EGHP premium payroll deductions, or bank statements, or personal receipts reflecting health insurance premiums paid if you did not use payroll deductions.

(5) Photocopied health insurance card with policy effective dates for each year eligible for Medicare but not enrolled.

(6) Explanation of Benefits, or "EOB," detailing the coverage provided to employees by your EGHP.

If you're still here and have definitely decided you will suspend Medicare at 65 and sign up after, you will be assigned a *Special Enrollment Period,* or in industry acronym jargon, your "SEP."

Your SEP is a certain and specific period of time, unique to your retirement situation, which determines your enrollment deadline. It is based on the month you will retire, and takes into account how long your employer group health plan (EGHP) will The details for signing up and starting Medicare after 65 are revealed in a later section of this book. **Turn to page 94...**

QUALIFYING QUESTIONS TO SIGN UP
AND START MEDICARE AFTER AGE 65

(1) If you are older than 65 and plan to retire --- will you also collect your Social Security Income benefits, or delay them until a later date?

    a. If 'YES,' you will have one less step when signing up and starting Medicare after 65

    b. If 'NO,' you will have one more step when signing up and starting Medicare after 65

(2) If you are older than 65 and planning to retire now --- have you been actively contributing to a Health Savings Account, or HSA, while actively employed since turning 65?

    a. If 'YES,' you have to stop contributions 6 months before signing up and starting Medicare due to the retroactivity clause, otherwise you will be assessed an IRA tax fine

    b. If 'NO,' you can disregard and move on

(3) If you are older than 65 and planning to retire now --- do you have the option of retiree health insurance from your employer (an Employer Group Health Plan, or EGHP)?

    a. If 'YES,' do they require you to sign up for Medicare Part A?

b. If 'YES,' do they require you to sign up for Medicare Part B?

c. If 'YES,' you will be forced to pay the Medicare monthly premium, in addition to the monthly price of your retiree plan, so make sure to compare coverage and costs between keeping your retiree plan or dropping it to pick a private Medicare plan. (More times than not, Medicare makes more financial sense).

d. If 'NO,' you <u>HAVE TO</u> sign up for Medicare.

(4) Does your Employer HR Department offer to fill out and file your Medicare forms, and coordinate your coverage for you? Or will you have to complete on your own?

a. If 'YES,' do they know the new rules, regulations, and requirements to ensure you do not have the typical 90-day processing delay?

b. If 'NO,' you will have your work cut out for you, so be sure to set aside some time to learn these new rules, regulations, and requirements.

(5) Do you know when your *Special Enrollment Period* begins? Or when your enrollment deadline expires?

(6) Will you qualify for "Premium-free" Medicare Part A? Or will you have to pay monthly for Medicare Part A?

(7) Everybody is assessed a monthly Medicare Part B premium based on your income from the last two years (ironically, likely your highest earning years while working). Do you know how much you will pay for your monthly Medicare Part B premium?

(8) Once your Medicare Part A and Part B have been activated, will you stay "bare" with Original Medicare, or choose to buy an additional private insurance plan?

(9) If you choose to buy an additional private insurance plan, do you understand what Medicare Part A covers, Medicare Part B covers, Medicare Part C covers, Medicare Part D covers, and the drastic differences between Medicare Supplement, Medigap, and Medicare Advantage?

(10)   Are you aware that there are now 11 different companies available for residents in WNY to compare and choose for private Medicare insurance (totaling over 201+) plans, each with different doctor networks, participating hospitals, preferred pharmacies and drug prices, as well as benefits beyond Medicare?

SMART STEPS TO SIGN UP AND START MEDICARE AFTER AGE 65

If you have found yourself here, you are older than age 65, planning to retire, and know you need to sign up and start Medicare. You likely have no other health insurance option in retirement other than Medicare.

This is the second most common situation I see with leading-edge baby boomers in Buffalo. You held out working until you reach the arbitrary "full retirement" age the Federal Government assigns you (either by choice 'cause you love your job, or by circumstance 'cause you need the money). Now the time has ticked down and you're ready to make your rendezvous with retirement.

If you have already read the previous section for those who know they need to sign up and start Medicare at 65, some of this will sound repetitive, but most of it will be new information, so pay close attention.

Signing up and starting Medicare after 65 is not simple...but I will do my best to make it simpler.

The Federal Government keeps changing their rules and regulations around how they want you to fill out and file your application forms, where they need to be submitted, and when they need to be submitted by.

I spend countless hours keeping up to date on these critical changes and have done all the hard work for you. Here's what you need to know...

Clearly understanding exactly when to apply for Medicare after 65 may be the single, most important thing you need to know because not getting this right can cost you thousands of dollars extra over your lifetime.

In fact, when you sign up and start Medicare after age 65, you are automatically assigned a late enrollment penalty, or "LEP." They assume you are at fault. Guilty until you can prove your innocence. All because you did not do what they wanted you to do, which is start paying them for Medicare right at 65 (it's a major money maker after all).

Your LEP is a monthly penalty, it's not a catch-up lump sum you payoff and move on. It is a lifetime penalty you will pay, over and over, each and every month, until the day you die. And it can increase the cost of your monthly Medicare premiums up a hefty 10% extra for every 12-month period that goes by from when you should have signed up for Medicare at 65 versus when you actually signed up for Medicare after 65.

But don't stress. If you pay close attention, I will explain to you the legal loophole to get out of this penalty.

To be technical, you should not apply for Medicare when you are retired, rather you should apply *before* you retire, so that your benefits will begin exactly on the first day of the next month, after your last day of work.

For you who suspended your Medicare at age 65 and now need to sign up later in life, you will be assigned a specific

Special Enrollment Period, or in industry acronym jargon, your "SEP".

Your SEP is a 4-month period that opens 2 months before the first day you need Medicare to start, and up to 63 days after you officially lose your Employer Group Health Plan, or EGHP. Obviously, the more proactive planning you can do, the better. Work plan ends and Medicare begins. No gap, no lapse, and no double coverage with work, or having to buy a costly COBRA plan to bridge the gap of poor planning. Smooth and seamless as expected. I like pictures, so hopefully this one helps...

60 Days To Apply For Medicare Proactively

RETIRE!

63 Days To Apply For Medicare Reactively

MEDICARE SMARTSTART STORY:
"NO PROOF PAUL"

The importance of pre-filing your "proof of credible coverage" forms cannot be overstated and stressed enough. To reveal to you the severity of not successfully doing these tasks, I'd like to share with you Paul's story and the struggle he and his wife Patty are now stuck with.

You see, Paul was self-employed. He owned and operated

his own construction business remodeling kitchens and bathrooms. Patty had stayed home to raise their three kids and acted as an unofficial employee, unpaid and off-the-books, to manage the money and the business benefits for Paul and the family.

Well, Paul was now nearing age 65 and the routine retirement conversations began. Retire, or not to retire? Social security now, or later? Is it even enough to live on, or not? Sign up for Medicare now, or suspend?

As the sole employee of the company, Paul had the business buying his health insurance, which allowed him to also provide health insurance to Patty, on an employee plus spouse plan.

But Patty being three (3) years younger than Paul, she would have no health insurance if Paul moved to Medicare because she was not an official, documented employee of the business.

So, with a quick check of what health insurance Patty could buy on her own for three years until she could sign up for Medicare, they were shocked to see how expensive individual health insurance is to buy on your own, outside of active employment. It seemed obvious that Paul would suspend Medicare at 65, keep working for three more years until both he and Patty could sign up and start Medicare at the same time.

After all, if the business keeps paying for their health insurance plan, it's a tax-deductible write-off, right?

Flash forward three years and I get a call from Patty to schedule a Medicare SmartStart Strategy Session with me for her and Paul to fill out and file their Medicare application forms.

After sharing their situation and getting answers to all their questions, we, unfortunately, figured out Paul would be paying a 39-month late enrollment penalty because, at first glance, the health insurance plan his business was buying for he and Patty did not meet the credible coverage requirements.

With the current Medicare Late Enrollment Penalty figures and formula, Paul would be paying, based on 39 months passing, an additional $40-$60 a month extra, in addition to the standard Medicare monthly price. That means an unnecessary $600 a year. And if the average life expectancy for men is about 85, Paul would be paying that $600 penalty for 17 years from the time he signed up and started Medicare at 68 until his projected possible death at 85. He would pay out-of-pocket more than $10,000 just on a foolish assumption.

Don't be like Paul, who had no proof of credible coverage. You have now learned 'which' move to make with Medicare and 'when' to make it. Your next step is to learn 'how' to fill out and file them correctly, on time, and without errors. **Turn to page 99...**

FILLING OUT AND FILING YOUR MEDICARE APPLICATION FORMS

As I made a careful caveat in my earlier promise to you, I've realized designing a DIY guide may not be the best way to save you time or uncertainty...and certainly not save your sanity.

The way I see it, sending you to sit at home, in isolation, with furrowed brow, would just leave you feeling fearful and frustrated and the last thing to be considered helpful.

But I think it's also important that I share with you all your options, not just cherry pick and curate the information. I included the good and bad, the easy and difficult, the simple and complicated, so that you can make your own choice.

The information I share with you on the next few pages will give you, in great detail, the five (5) different ways you can fill out and file your Medicare application forms. Four requiring your sleeves rolled up and some elbow grease and the fifth, alternative option, will seem almost effortless, with little to no effort required on your part.

STRESSED SENDING BY SNAIL MAIL

Certainly, the most time-consuming and tedious of choices, you can still send your Medicare application by mail, but it comes with significant stress and struggle.

You will need to request hardcopy, printed Medicare application paperwork to fill out by hand and file with the Social Security Central Processing Facility, sent by paid postage out of your pocket.

When (if) received, Central Processing personnel will qualify the quality and accuracy of your application.

If found to be correct and complete, without errors and without missing, incomplete, or inaccurate information, your forms will be forwarded to the smaller Social Security office assigned to your file based by your zip code for processing and activation approval.

This process typically takes more than 3 months to go through from start to finish before you have confirmation of Medicare coverage.

Clearly, an excellent example of government efficiency.

The biggest challenge with this choice is if an error is found, or something incomplete or inaccurate is in question, they send all your Medicare forms back to you by snail mail, just like how you sent it to them (with an instruction sheet on what to fix and how).

By the time you're done playing all this back-and-forth ping-pong, your Medicare may not start on the day you want or need which is why many folks have stopped using the snail mail method.

FRUSTRATED WITH PHONE ROBOTS

A seemingly smart solution to save you from all the snail mail stress and struggle, but a failed attempt. Most humans tend to get frustrated trying to talk with phone robots and feel like they are getting nowhere.

If you'd prefer not to fill out your forms by hand, a Medicare phone application is available. When first introduced, the idea was for you to call the National Social Security Call Center within your Initial Enrollment Period pre-65, push in your zip code, and be instantly connected to a courteous federal employee who would complete your Medicare application correctly right then and there.

In reality, the government over-promised and under-delivered. Social Security has been understaffed and continues to be post-pandemic, unable to handle the call volume with 10,000 baby boomers projected to be turning 65 every day presumably past the year 2030.

If you do decide to call, be prepared to probably be on hold for hours at a time. They do not allow you to apply over the phone on that first call. Your first call is to request a "phone interview," which is when they will go through the forms with you over the phone. It is a prescheduled and preset time that *they* call you --- usually early. You miss the call; they don't try twice. You have to call back, start all over, and reschedule a new phone interview.

Currently, phone interviews are being scheduled 13-17 weeks in advance so you need to time it right and place your initial call almost 6 months pre-65, so you can schedule your phone interview inside your Initial Enrollment Period to avoid delays, gaps, or lapses in coverage.

AGGRAVATED BY APPOINTMENT

Previous to the chaotic circus that COVID created, you used to be able to walk right into any Social Security office and get human help --- and helped immediately --- on that very same day. It wasn't the most speedy or exciting experience, much like the DMV, but you got your number, waited your turn, and got done what you went there to do.

Like the understaffing issue causing the phone fiasco, many Federal employees are still allowed to work remotely, enjoying taxpayer funded half days with full pay, and little to no accountability or activity monitoring.

This "new normal" has also affected the ability of the Social

Security offices to staff appropriately to accommodate those who wish, want, and probably prefer to walk in and speak with someone about applying for Medicare, Social Security supplemental income, or both.

To my recent requests, both the Buffalo Social Security offices and West Seneca Social Security offices continue to keep limited, to no, walk-in hours available.

If truly your preference and priority, you are allowed to call the National Call Center and rather than request a "phone interview," you can request an in-person appointment. The location you will be assigned is based on your zip code and appointment availability is based on the staffing situation of the day.

Similar to scheduling phone interviews, in-person appointments have a long and lengthy delay in availability and access, with most recent reports showing 14-20 weeks depending on limitations of location.

CHALLENGED USING THE COMPUTER

For those who feel comfortable and capable with computers, this might be your best option. But before you get excited, things aren't always what they seem. Let me explain...

Prior to 2022, Medicare and Social Security both offered and operated their own individual secure websites: medicare.gov and ssa.gov. Each site required a unique username and password to create an access account. The two sites did not talk to one another.

In 2022, a new government sponsored site was released under the domain name login.gov. It promised to provide a "single secure sign on with private account access to participating government agencies." Sounds good but causing more new problems than fixing old ones.

Two things to consider: the first, (1) if you have already created a username and password on either of the legacy sites (medicare.gov or ssa.gov), you will not be able to create new account access using login.gov. You can try, but when you type in your social security number during the two-step identity verification, it will give you an error message that your social security number is already linked to another account. The second, (2) is the security settings on your home or personal computer likely do not meet the government minimum requirements. (I even went above and beyond to get special software installed in the office so we can take care of this step for Medicare SmartStart Program participants).

If the new login.gov site *does* work for you without a hitch or hiccup, excellent!

Using the online Medicare application prevents you from doing anything wrong. It does not let you move forward unless everything is complete and correct. And you get a real-time receipt of submission and controlled confirmation number.

The only problem is I've never had anyone call me to

confirm they were able to use the new login.gov site successfully. Maybe you'll have better luck and be the first?

DELIGHTFULLY DONE-FOR-YOU

We've come to a fork in the road. Some readers will still follow the old, outdated, traditional ways of years past. Which you now definitively know are all just different ways of doing the same thing.

And if you're like most readers who have gotten to this point, you're probably at the place of feeling like everything I just explained seems to be unhelpful and useless.

After telling and teaching you about your limited and lacking options, you might be thinking there just doesn't seem to be any real, reliable resources when it comes to signing up and starting Medicare. And I agree.

Now, imagine if you could wave a magic wand and free yourself from having to spend your own scarce free time, never needing to do anything yourself or having to think about the one thing you don't want to think about...Medicare.

I can make that happen. It's what my free Medicare SmartStart Program is all about.

So, if you're interested, keep reading to learn about why most people struggle with Medicare, but you won't...

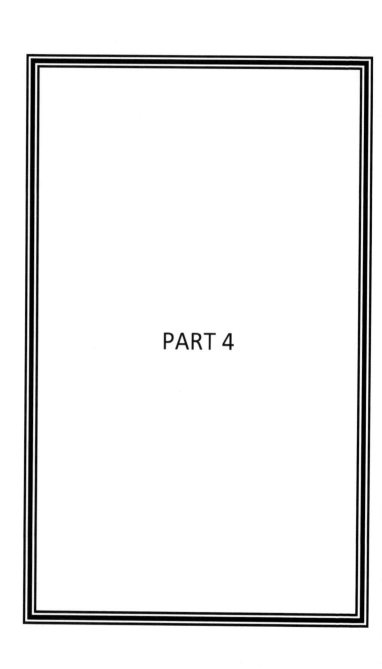

PART 4

NOW WHAT?

**SmartStart
Smart Tip**

"Life's tough. It's tougher
if you're stupid."
John Wayne

"Medicare's tough. It's tougher
if you don't ask for help."
Andrew Hibbard

WHY MOST PEOPLE STRUGGLE WITH MEDICARE, BUT YOU WON'T

Starting Medicare smartly may very well be one of the most important decisions you will have to make in your lifetime. A decision that deserves special attention. Maybe even more than you think to give it.

Can I share a secret with you?

I personally do not find Medicare *that* difficult but it's likely because it's all I do day in and day out. You don't. Which makes me comfortable with the needed and necessary conversation having learned the knowledge and earned the know-how to feel confident. You have not. So, I get why you feel overwhelmed, but to be brutally honest, we've only just scratched the surface.

Typically, the first question everybody wants to ask when I work with them is *"what insurance plan should I pick?"*

You may be thinking the same thing, however, that is cart

before the horse stuff. It's like focusing on the finish line before we even step onto the field.

So, I'm sorry to disappoint that this book does not even attempt to take you down the long and winding road of sorting through the sea of insurance companies, explain the technical translation skills you will need to figure out all the fine print between plans, or how to accurately compare costs and coverage so you can get the very best plan, at the very best price, and enjoy the very best bang for your buck, the very first time you buy your private Medicare insurance.

Forget all that for a second. Right now, we only need to focus on STEP 1: To definitely decide whether you need to, have to, or not to sign up and start Medicare at 65...and how to go about filling out and filing your forms correctly, on time, and without errors.

Only the smartest people find a way to make complicated things --- uncomplicated.

You may have already heard all the horror stories of just how time-consuming and soul-sucking dealing with Medicare is.

I think it's extremely unreasonable for you to be expected to fill out and file the proper forms, at the proper time, in the proper way?!

Without any instructions, you have to accept your own assumptions or hit-or-miss guesses as the only way to do things. And that's not fair!

The problem isn't with you, it's with the information you have.

You see, many throughout WNY keep playing a game of "monkey see – monkey do" and don't understand that just signing up and starting Medicare the same way other people have done doesn't make it smart...it only makes it common.

The mass majority think Medicare is confusing and complicated...and that's just the way it is. That Medicare is difficult to understand, and you must struggle and suffer through it, like others have done, and continue to do.

So, if you want to make Medicare simpler and easier, you don't need another generic "Welcome To Medicare" letter or any more Medicare mass-marketing mail.

What you do need is a smart, sure-fire way to get started; in other words, a step-by-step program that takes away all the guesswork, without you really having to do any of the work.

And if you're willing to forget the traditional way of doing it all yourself --- and do things differently --- I promise you can shortcut hours / days / weeks off the whole process.

Would You Rather Walk Or Be Driven?

Here's what I mean...

Just how <u>EASY</u> do you want to make it to get signed up and started with Medicare?

Do you want to walk and take the slow, plodding, 'find your own way' route to your destination?

Or would you rather BE DRIVEN DIRECTLY and enjoy the FAST, EFFICIENT, and TIME-SAVING chauffeured concierge experience?

Yes, you'll have to invest a small amount of your time and spend about an hour with me, so you can share your situation, but you'll have the luxury of getting an exclusive experience, get personal service and attention, and get things DONE RIGHT and in WAY LESS TIME, while others continue to stress and struggle.

And who doesn't want that?

Plus, you'll benefit from having an expert driver driving you the entire way, so you don't have to worry or stress about a thing.

And isn't that the way we'd all like to get where we need to go...quickly and easily SAVED FROM ALL THE STRUGGLE AND STRIFE? That's exactly how I look at signing up and starting with Medicare...

You could walk and try to figure it all out on your own, spending a ton of your time thinking about the one thing you don't actually want to be thinking about at all (Medicare)...

Or you could save yourself all that time, uncertainty, and maybe even your sanity by taking the FAST TRACK.

Sounds good, right?

Now is the time for you to choose...

TWO CHOICES, BUT ONLY
ONE MAKES SENSE

Most people assume I mean, either sign up for Medicare at 65 or suspend Medicare and sign up after 65, some other time, later in life. And while that is a choice you need to make; I have a different thought on your choices --- which applies to everyone in every situation.

Let me explain...

As you approach 65, you do in fact have two (2) choices, sign up for Medicare or not --- and I truthfully don't really know what you should do until we get together, sit down, you share your situation, and we talk things out. (FYI: For most, signing up for Medicare does actually make more financial sense at 65, even if you'll keep working).

But whether you need to sign up for Medicare at 65 or not, there's a much more important choice I want to talk about. An important choice that might be the single, most important thing deciding your success with Medicare or not. That is, should you risk trying to tackle Medicare by doing-it-yourself or should you ask for help?

The way I see it, you can either spend your hours/days/weeks in isolation, relying on your own assumptions and hit-or-miss guesses wondering if you are doing things right or risking messing up your Medicare, just to do it all twice, or worse, making a costly mistake that will follow you for life.

Or you can rely on my time-saving shortcut and proven step-by-step process hundreds of other folks in WNY have already relied on to make their move to Medicare simpler and easier.

Why stress yourself out trying to figure it out on your own? I have a much better way, I assure you.

Think of it like this...

When you own or lease a vehicle, there are certain decisions that need to be made when a warning sign shows you something needs to be done. Such as, an indicator light will flash on the dashboard, or you'll start hearing a whizz, whirr, or clunk because the oil needs a changin', or a wheel bearing is going bad.

That's the same kind of sign you get from Medicare when they mail you out their information packet that you'll soon be 65 and need to sign up. Consider that the dashboard light flashing is telling you something needs to be done.

Now, the decision you need to make, the special attention

you need to give, is not about what problem needs to be solved, but rather *how* the problem will be solved, right?

Some brave do-it-yourselfers will certainly look forward to taking the whole weekend to work on things themselves. But they need to have all the right tools to do so successfully. Floor jack, jack stands, rachets, wrenches, specialty sockets, and who knows what else.

They willingly spend their free time and have a desire to deal with doing those things directly. But I'd be willing to wager that's not the norm anymore.

In today's times, the mass majority of people are making a call to a mechanic. A qualified professional who can diagnose and prescribe a solution to the problem...and do all the work for you.

That's how I think about you signing up and starting with Medicare. If you are someone who doesn't have the time or the desire to deal with Medicare directly, imagine me as your "Medicare Mechanic."

For a large handful of folks, it seems obvious to ask for help, and for a small group, they are stubborn do-it-yourselfers that come hell or high water, they would rather fail by themselves than be successful by asking for help.

Only you know which camp you fall in.

This isn't going to be a lengthy discussion on the importance of asking for help when you don't feel confident because you lack the knowledge and the know-how --- especially with things like Medicare --- where most mistakes, when you make them, cannot be corrected and follow you for life.

A recent Centers For Medicare Services (CMS) study stated, "An overall lack of knowledge about the Medicare enrollment process, costs, and benefits are putting millions of people who are turning 65 and eligible to enroll in Medicare at potential risk of lapses with insurance coverage, excess surcharges, penalties, and wasted spending, not to mention missed opportunities for critical benefits and services."

With that information, I wonder if you had to bet your life on 100% certainty that you are doing everything right with Medicare, would you really risk doing it yourself?

Probably not.

But for those diehard DIY'ers, I give you my blessing if you want to paint your living room walls without help. If you make a mistake, you can just paint over it. You try growing a vegetable garden on your own and you let a plant die, no harm no foul. Just dig it up and plant a new seed and start over. It's not that easy to get a "re-do" with the Federal Government.

Now, I know it seems like a lot of information we went through, and it can feel like you're drinking from a firehose. Especially if you weren't expecting how complex, complicated, and just downright confusing Medicare will be.

So, if you got through all this stuff in one sitting, kudos to you! And if it took you a little longer, at least you stuck with it!

I still argue that nobody actually wants to think about Medicare...let alone spend their free time to understand it so they feel more educated on the matter.

Would you agree?

What I think people really want is to feel *confident*. Confident they:

- Smartly decided whether they should sign up and start Medicare at 65...or suspend until later in life
- Have done everything required with Medicare on time, correctly, and without errors
- Will avoid any late enrollment penalties if they do decide to sign up for Medicare after age 65
- Pick an insurance plan that won't make them refinance their house when an unexpected medical event occurs, so they won't go into debt over all the big bills
- Can enjoy retirement and freely travel outside of NY without worry if they will be able to receive the care that is needed, at an affordable price
- Are financially protected and have some sort of cap on their out-of-pocket healthcare costs, so they don't ruin their credit or go into collections
- Don't need to change doctors from the ones they have been seeing for years, and prefer to keep seeing in the future, just because certain companies only allow certain doctors

I'm sure you have similar wants and wishes, and the most important thing is making sure you know what you need to do and when you need to do it, so you can see the results you want.

Hopefully, reading this short, helpful book has helped you make up your mind whether you feel I am "your guy." The one you'd trust to take away the "scare" of Medicare and make such a challenging chore...easier and almost effortless for you.

If you are telling yourself, *"YES! This guy gets me. I don't have the time or desire to deal with any of this Medicare stuff myself,"* then you might also be asking, *"what the heck do I do next?"*

Well, I'm so glad you asked...

Just about anyone can follow along and do what others are already doing, but remember, that doesn't make it smart...it only makes it common. And you're not part of the common crowd, right? You're a Medicare Smart S.T.A.R.T.E.R.

So, if that's you, I'd love to hear from you.

Now is the time to discover my free Medicare SmartStart Program and join the previous 850+ Western New Yorkers who have already put this proven program to work for them, too.

And, as a valued book reader, I've put together a very special, no cost, no obligation, very limited-time offer just for YOU!

All you have to do is take the next step...

THE NEXT STEP

If you have arrived at this page after reading everything in this book, then thank you and congratulations. I hope everything I have explained about my Medicare SmartStart Program sounds like something you would find helpful.

Now is where the common crowd stops. They will nod their head and tell themselves they need to take advantage of this opportunity, but they will take no action.

I encourage you to be different.

Just by making it to the end of this book tells me you might have been inspired and hopeful throughout these pages...maybe even excited there seems to be a way to save you from all the stress of trying to tackle Medicare on your own?

If that's the type of thing you're looking for and would like, I invite you to put my proven Medicare SmartStart Program to work for you and schedule your free Medicare SmartStart Strategy Session with me.

It's how I help people just like you.

Our time together will be a quick "get acquainted" opportunity for us, lasting about 60 minutes, so you can share your situation and I can see how I can best help you.

We'll have a casual conversation where I will be able to answer all your Medicare questions and we will put your step-by-step plan in place.

The first focus for me is making sure to take away all your fears and frustrations about Medicare, so before you head home, I will create a customized "myMedicare SmartPath" Guide Map tailored to you for the taking, all free of charge and at absolutely no cost whatsoever as my gift (a $20.00 value).

You'll leave with simple and easy-to-understand steps, from start to finish, so you'll know exactly how to get where you need to go with Medicare. As easy as 1-2-3.

Sound good?

NOTE: This is <u>NOT</u> a sales meeting of any sort. In fact, I have nothing to sell you, and there is no legal way for you to give me any money. Our time together is purely educational, so no need to wonder about what to expect.

And, if interested, I'd strongly suggest you put this book down right now and schedule your free Medicare SmartStart Strategy Session before you become busy and forget.

Especially because, while yes, I am offering free access to

my complete Medicare SmartStart Program to all book readers, there is a strong sense of urgency I should also share.

I understand it can be hard thinking you have to spend your time worrying about Medicare while still working, and still have time for the things you enjoy, plus finding all the time you'd like to give to your friends and family...especially those special moments with your grandkids.

I want to save you all that time from the painstaking Medicare process and procedures, and my free Medicare SmartStart Program will give you a tremendous unfair advantage --- often overlooked by others --- which leads them to unnecessary stress, struggle, and drastically less than desirable results, while you'll have no worries in the world.

But as much as I want to help everyone who is interested, I realistically cannot meet with the hundreds in WNY who request time with me each and every year.

Most weeks I have Medicare articles I am asked to write, employer events to present privately, and seminar invites wishing me to speak, which can severely restrict my schedule. Plus, I have three kids and I won't compromise being home for dinner at the table together, so I have to draw a line.

Because of this, I only schedule about 8-10 Medicare SmartStart Strategy sessions each week, which works out to 32-36 every month due to the complexity and coordination with Medicare on your behalf (Doing everything with Medicare for you is a time-consuming task, but I'm sure you'd agree better me doing it all than you, right?)

My free Medicare SmartStart Program is the most popular service I offer, and those 8-10 weekly time slots fill up quick. Many of them are pre-filled from other people who requested this book in previous months, who have been referred to me through our friends and family *FASTPASS* program, from strategic partners within physician's practices around town, or our local community outreach efforts. I can only encourage you not to procrastinate.

Remember, 65 is the new 45, and as an active adult, I know you've likely got a big, long bucket list to enjoy, so securing and saving your scarce free time should be important to you.

If you feel like you don't know where to start with Medicare, or you don't have the time or desire to deal with Medicare directly...this is the easiest and simplest way for you to take away all the stress of trying to tackle Medicare on your own and get back to enjoying whatever it is you enjoy most --- golfing, gardening, going to Disney, grandkids --- or whatever else floats your boat.

You definitely don't want to miss out on this.

All you have to do is schedule your free Medicare SmartStart Strategy Session with me to get started. It's that simple.

Dorothy had Glenda.

Luke had Yoda.

Who will be your guide to help you start Medicare smartly?

I have tried to make it as easy and effortless as I can for you with three (3) convenient ways to work together.

HOW TO SCHEDULE YOUR FREE MEDICARE SMARTSTART STRATEGY SESSION WITH ME

Visit our secure scheduling page at
MedicareSmartStartWNY.com

Or Call **716-833-0252** Or Scan

**SmartStart
Smart Tip**

"It's not about how smart you are,
it's about how are you smart."
Howard Gardner

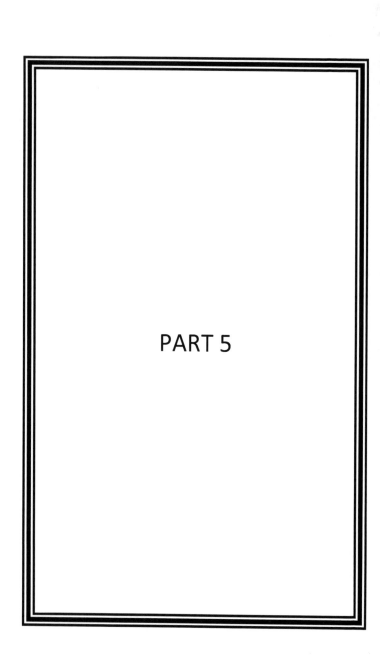

PART 5

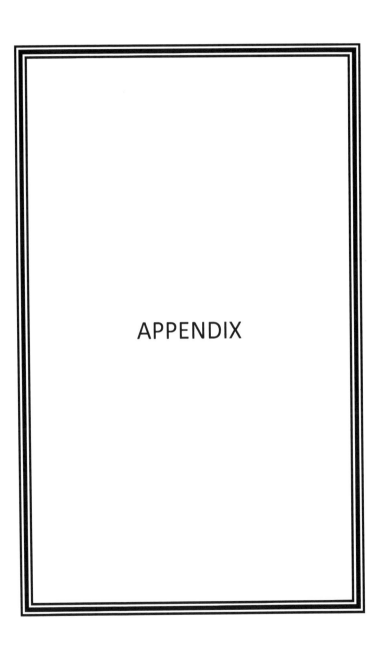

APPENDIX

SmartStart
Smart Tip

"Entrepreneurs and their small enterprise
are responsible for almost all economic
growth in the country. We, the American
public, have a duty to support them, to
see the communities we share prosper."
Ronald Reagan

ONLY SOME SUPPORT LOCAL SMALL BUSINESS, WILL YOU?

Signing up and starting Medicare does not have to be the oft dreaded experience that so many WNY'ers share stories about. One of the best ways to make the entire process easier, simpler, almost effortless, and even somewhat stress-free is to rely on a reputable local Medicare specialist instead of trying to tackle it all at home, online, or worse, walking into a corporate insurance company sales center.

You want to research and review someone, someplace, somewhere with specific and specialized resources and services for *starting* Medicare (the signing up part of filling out and filing your federal forms) and stay away from any and all places that are attempting to get your attention as part of the insurance sales process.

Remember, a Medicare Smart S.T.A.R.T.E.R. prefers and prioritizes being educated not solicited, which likely means a local small business offering general and generic information will be much better in supporting your success than a corrupt corporate sales center, a bribed, bonused and bought-off broker, or the coercive tele-sale scammers calling from out-of-state.

The following are some smart, ever important, and extremely impactful reasons why you should seek out a local Medicare service if you're looking to support local small business in Buffalo.

RELYING ON A REPUTABLE LOCAL SMALL BUSINESS MATTERS BECAUSE YOUR LOCAL COMMUNITY MATTERS TO YOU

If you are like the 99% of other WNY'ers I work with, you were born and bred in Buffalo. Maybe you're like me, born in Buffalo but might have found a reason to move away and once gone, found a more compelling reason to return. Seems everybody born in Buffalo comes back to Buffalo.

Either way, for a variety of reasons, how you support your hometown directly and undeniably affects everything concerning the community and its success and sustainability.

More often than not, your decisions should be based on supporting local business, first. And in a lot of cases, the local small business owner built that business because of a personal problem, and their solution ended up having a huge impact helping others through the same struggle and strife.

Because they have learned how to create a solution to solve their own problem first, they have also earned the ability to anticipate your same and similar pain points which guarantees you'll be taken care of in the best way possible to ensure you never have to go through what they had to go through.

A LOCAL SMALL BUSINESS CAN PROVIDE YOU A MUCH BETTER FACE-TO-FACE EXPERIENCE VERSUS THE FACELESS EXPERIENCE YOU'LL HAVE OVER THE PHONE OR ONLINE

There's nothing wrong with phone robots or consulting a computer for answers. You might actually get your answers quicker in some cases, but my concern is what happens afterward?

If you are anything like everyone else nearing the age of 65, you created a checklist of basic Medicare questions you believe should be asked and answered. And that's smart.

You may be thinking it'll be super simple and straightforward to call a 1-800-number over-the-phone or go online and get answers based on those questions you thought to ask. True. But only the ones you think to ask then and there.

The phone robot, or potential real person who astonishingly answers, does not --- and will not --- volunteer additional answers to questions that you DID NOT ask but you probably *should* have.

They aren't proactive. They won't plot and plan your step-by-step path, from start to finish like when face-to-face.

Yes, you'll get answers to your first round of questions, feel better and hang up. You'll take time on your own to dive deeper into what they told you and another ten questions come up. So, you have to call back, get a different person, and in all your anger and annoyance, reluctantly retell and share your situation again, and start all over with someone else.

Showing your support and trusting a local small business will avoid these aggravations, headaches, and hassles. You can call the same person, at the same place, and pick up right where you left off. And, working together on a first name basis gives you the upper hand to hold them accountable for their actions.

Personal responsibility is a thing of the past dealing over-the-phone or online, but it is alive and well within the local small business community. Reputation and reviews are the two things that can never be taken away or replaced in a local small business.

YOU HAVE TO SPEND TIME DEALING WITH MEDICARE ANYWAYS, SO WHY NOT SPEND IT SUPPORTING A LOCAL SMALL BUSINESS

Regardless of if you determine and decide it's a smart decision to sign up and start Medicare at 65 --- or suspend

Medicare to sign up later in life after 65 --- you are spending a good amount of time dealing with making this decision.

Many, if not most, spend a decent number of days online trying to figure out all the fine print only to then spend a handful of hours on the phone with Social Security. This soul-sucking process can cost you 20+ hours of your scarce free time, to still feel like you haven't gotten anywhere.

If you search and seek out a local small business who can save you all of that time, and give you clear, credible, concise, and correct answers, why not spend your time letting them do all the dirty work with Medicare so you don't have to?

COMMUNITY COMRADERY CAN BE CREATED SUPPORTING LOCAL SMALL BUSINESS

Today, more than ever, there is a culture war across the country, directly divided by ideals and identities, and you, the consumer, directly determine which business will survive, thrive, or die.

As of late, I have gone out of my way to research people and places I relate to, and will get along with, before I buy something, or do business with them.

There is a significant advantage and noticeable enhanced and enriched experience when I diligently do this type of preliminary planning. There is an immediate and instant rapport and relationship based on common convictions and verified values. The conversation is like catching up with an old friend without all the angst and anxiety that comes with meeting someone new and unknown.

With local small business, there is a much higher percentage that the owner is involved in the day-to-day operations and will personally know *you*, know *you* by name, and know *your* needs, as well as you knowing them by name and considering them a close friend, like family.

Many times, when new Medicare SmartStart Program participants are referred, we can effectively and efficiently get the mundane and mandatory Medicare out of the way in the first few minutes, and spend more time talking my Air Force awards & decorations, some of my Fire Service displays, my wife's Broadway performances working with Disney, or most often, our shared love of America and my limited edition "Republican Club" artwork that was hand-drawn by artist, Andy Thomas.

SUPPORTING LOCAL SMALL BUSINESS HELPS SOMEONE ELSE SURVIVE, PAY THEIR BILLS AND COVER BASIC EXPENSES, NOT BUYING A CORPORATE CEOS NEW SPEEDBOAT

It's an astonishing fact many fail to take interest in and ignore but being in business --- especially a small, family run business --- has its challenges when you're up against big corporate conglomerates.

Every dollar earned has to be spent 5 different ways. And when the cost of doing business is covered first, there isn't much meat left on the bones to pay your payroll or support a family. There's typically more month at the end of the money.

In fact, the average salary for a self-employed, small business owner is only $49,804 a year, according to the U.S. Small Business Association. And while for some that may seem like a lot, or at least livable, think about how many small business owners are husband-wife tag-team duos, who likely share the salary the business is able to pay. What they are paid has to be split in two, so it doesn't go as far. (I know speaking from experience because that's how it works for my wife and I in our business).

So, who and what do you want your time and efforts supporting? A mom and dad trying to pay their bills, cover basic expenses, and save a little on the side to dine out at dinner once in a while…or another corporate CEOs second vacation home or new speed boat?

THE SURVIVAL OF LOCAL SMALL BUSINESS SHOULD MATTER BECAUSE YOU MATTER

You may not even realize the seismic shift your habits and behaviors can create in the economics of the local community. Some people don't care to consider these certain factors, but I believe most Baby Boomers, brought up on traditional American values, would make some significant changes if they were better informed.

Sometimes, people have the "I'm only one person, what difference can I make?" attitude. It is utterly untrue and fundamentally wrong. We all <u>DO</u> make a difference in what we decide --- sometimes positive, sometimes negative --- and those choices all have some kind of impact and imprint in our lives and the lives of others --- sometimes positive, sometimes negative --- especially in our own hometown.

Understand this universal truth: everything we do matters to someone, in some way, somewhere.

Think of things that matter like this...

- Your footprints (where you've been and where you go next)
- Your fingerprints (what you've done and what you do next)
- Places you choose to go (and places you choose not to go)
- People you help (people you choose not to help)
- Who you decide to trust (who you decide not to trust)

Literally, the list is endless, and can include the money you choose to spend versus money you choose not to spend (which will determine if you have a lot of *stuff*, but little to no savings for a well-prepared financial future).

Or, even where you spend money to support and where you don't spend money to not support (like shopping on Amazon to make them stronger while making local business weaker).

LOCAL SMALL BUSINESS IS BETTER FOR YOU

"Shop Local," and "Support Small Business In Buffalo" are both key phrases we've all heard around town that are finally bringing back the importance and attention it deserves, long forgotten from the good 'ole days pre-internet where members within close knit communities depended and relied upon one another.

Many things innovated with the internet age has made access to stuff easier and simpler. (To which I'd argue has made everyone fatter, dumber, and distracted --- but a conversation for another day).

Wider selection of consumer goods delivered directly to your door. Groceries to go where you can order online, never set foot in a supermarket, and someone else will carry the bags to your car. Even secondary schooling and course curriculums can be taken through the computer. But for some reason, Medicare has not been made more accessible or more easily understandable.

Your local Medicare specialist offers you a significant advantage when you need answers and are looking for a solution. You can share your situation with a person who actually has an interest in you and your issues, giving you an immediate diagnosis of sorts and instant prescription to solve your perceived problem.

Personal touch has been so lost in the commotion of computer dependency. Signing up and starting Medicare can cause such stress and struggle, so anything or anyone making a more pleasant and positive experience should be valued as priceless.

Trying to deal with Medicare directly, either over the phone or online can never compete with the caring and considerate, one-on-one, face-to-face, loving interactions from a local small business.

Of course, I do not believe you should blindly patronize any and all local small business --- there are shysters and scammers corrupted in the WNY community, too.

I don't think any local small business should expect you to choose them over their competition. That would be an entitlement mindset, which I am not about. You work for what you want. Nobody owes you anything.

But I would be remiss if I didn't ask for the opportunity to earn your trust and showcase all I have to offer you as your personal starting Medicare specialist.

It's entirely possible we will even bump into each other during casual moments out in the community: dinner out, pumping gas, or shopping at Wegmans on the weekend. I recognize this, and realize an unhappy customer, who feels unhelped, is not the person I want to be confronted by, so I go to great lengths to not only set you up for success with Medicare *before* you sign up and start but also always bend over backward to exceed your highest expectations and make things right if something unexpected happens.

I believe many of the problems in America could be fixed if everyone supported their local small businesses and local communities more. If local communities are supported better, they are made stronger. Which makes the town stronger. And the county stronger. And the state stronger. And with stronger states, a stronger country.

So, ask yourself, where will you turn to for help when you want to start Medicare smartly?

RESOURCES

If you are turning 65 in the next 3-4 months, it is URGENT you schedule your free Medicare SmartStart Strategy Session sooner than later: **MedicareSmartStartWNY.com**

If you are turning 65 in the next 6-12 months, you can learn more about the free Medicare SmartStart Program in WNY and request a complimentary, no cost information kit: **MedicareSmartStartWNY.com/Info**

If you would like helpful insider information about Medicare, along with access to critical checklists and some time-saving tips they don't tell you, or want you to know, please take advantage of my "Prepare For Medicare Pre-Planning Pack" as a valuable bonus gift for readers of this book: **StartingMedicareSmartly.com/Bonus**

If you would like to ask some quick questions, and prefer to speak to a happy, helpful human, rather than reading and researching yourself, please call me at: **716 . 833 . 0252**

(P.S. my wife Lyndsey will answer, so just let her know you've got this book and she'll give you a little preferential priority over the general public)

ABOUT THE AUTHOR
ANDREW L. HIBBARD

A ndrew L Hibbard is a 10-year veteran of the United States Air Force. Born in Buffalo, he shifted from serving his country to serving his hometown community and has become a best-selling author, an expert Medicare advisor, successful agency owner, and one of the top advocates in the Western New York area.

As a pioneering industry leader, he has been a sought-after guest-speaker on WECK Radio *Senior Matters*, an exclusive contributor to *Forever Young* Magazine, and the author of the most popular and preferred Medicare reference guidebook for Erie County residents, *Starting Medicare Smartly*.

In 2015, Andrew founded Medicare Management of WNY with his wife, Lyndsey, to be the first "anti-insurance agency" of its kind statewide, with intention to provide residents throughout WNY a brand-new service prioritizing "education over solicitation" free from any insurance company incentives and conflict of interest.

Soon after, the positive impact and popularity of his private Medicare planning processes and procedures gave birth to the "Medicare SmartStart Program," a nationally recognized resource, offered as a free step-by-step program which has now helped more than 850+ WNY'ers make signing up and starting Medicare simpler, easier, seemingly stress-free and almost effortless.

The innovative strategies of his Medicare SmartStart Program are trusted by well-known WNY companies and their retirees like *Fisher Price, MOOG, Wishbone, Catholic Charities, Amherst Schools, Clarence Schools, Perry's Ice Cream* and others which cannot be named due to legal liabilities.

Andrew lives in Akron, NY with his wife, their three kids: two daughters, Charlie and Chloe, and son Chase, along with their Australian Cattle Dog, Ollie. He enjoys skiing, camping, carpentry, and supporting local community activities. To date, he and his wife have donated 10% of their total business earnings directly back into WNY community causes through his continued "Charitable Giving Commitment" pledge.

To learn more about Andrew and how he and his wife Lyndsey are changing the Medicare industry for the better, from the inside out, please visit their website at: **www.WNYmedicare.org**

ABOUT THE MEDICARE SMARTSTART PROGRAM

The Medicare SmartStart Program was created specifically for people who don't have the time or desire to deal with Medicare directly on their own, who want to shortcut the typical time it takes to sign up and start, and prefer someone else to do it all for them.

While this book, *Starting Medicare Smartly* will certainly get you pointed in the right direction, it isn't going to get you feeling 100% confident --- or 100% competent --- in knowing everything you need to do about Medicare (or how to do it).

I can share story after story about folks who are 6 months away from turning 65, know they need to start thinking about what to do with Medicare, so they ask for a free copy of this book but fast forward 90 days and they still have done nothing. They haven't even opened the book.

Often, when I follow up with them, they are thankful to have received it but set it aside to come back to another day, only to become busy and forget...or they've quickly realized they have more to worry about with Medicare than they're willing to handle on their own.

That's where my Medicare SmartStart Program can help. And the exact reason why I'm willing to personally meet with you, so you get the results you want, without having to really do any of the work.

Now, more than 850+ Western New Yorkers have been put through my Medicare SmartStart Program, and it has widely become the most popular way to get signed up and started with Medicare in WNY.

"The proof is in the pudding," they say. Here's a snapshot of our lounge area showcasing the most recent additions of smiling, satisfied participants that have successfully gone through my Medicare SmartStart Program:

WHAT PEOPLE ARE SAYING

If you're interested in seeing what others around town are saying, participants aren't just simply satisfied --- they're head over heels *in love* with my can't-miss, must-have, hold you by the hand Medicare SmartStart Program!

I've included just some of the 250+ raving 5-star reviews for you to read from our Google Business page, Facebook, and third-party rating and ranking site, Trust Pilot:

A Local Treasure That More Folks Turning 65 Need To Discover!

"I was so thrilled to discover "Mr. Medicare" at Medicare Management of WNY after I entered the Medicare Maze and couldn't find my way out. All anxiety was relieved when Andrew explained their expertise on everything Medicare.

They made the experience easy and saved us so much money. Andrew and Lyndsey helped me find my way out of the maze so that I could retire. There is no fee for their services. I have recommended them to several of my friends. Those that followed up and contacted them have returned to thank me. Why wouldn't I recommend them to the people I care about? I consider Andrew and Lyndsey a local treasure that more folks turning 65 need to discover. I encourage you to call them--you will not regret it!"

---John & Marcia Donahue (Springville, NY)

They Treat You Like Family

"Great people to deal with. Extremely knowledgeable and very friendly. They treat you like family."

---Jim & Karen Saxer (Williamsville, NY)

Speak With Them Before You Do Anything With Medicare

"Andrew was extremely helpful and gave me information I never had before which directly helped me make better decisions. It is a wonderful service and I highly recommend you speak with them before you do anything with Medicare"

---Peggy Attardo (East Amherst, NY)

They Take Care Of Everything For You
--- And At No Cost

"They can answer any and all questions that you have concerning Medicare. We wouldn't go anywhere else. It's a huge relief knowing they take care of everything for you --- and at no cost to you. Something we were not looking forward to turned into a pleasurable experience. They are the nicest and most knowledgeable to entrust with managing your healthcare needs. We'd like to give them more than 5 stars if it was an option. Thanks again for all you've done for us.

---Paul & Judy Scott (Tonawanda, NY)

Andrew Took The Time To Guide Me
Through The Enrollment Process

"Signing up for Medicare looks pretty confusing at first glance. After meeting with Andrew at Medicare Management of WNY, they answered all of my questions right then and there! Andrew took the time to guide me through the enrollment process and what to consider when picking my insurance plan. I had helpful reminders at certain check points, and they oversaw all of the details. Great, friendly people to work with and very knowledgeable about the entire Medicare process."

---Paul Kropovitch (Cheektowaga, NY)

Andrew Is A Medicare Genius!

"Andrew is a Medicare genius! If you don't consult with him before you turn 65, and before you sign up for anything, you might be doing the wrong thing at the wrong time. And when it comes time to pick your plan, you might not select a plan that's just right for you and pay more than is necessary. He knows all the "ins" and the "outs" of the Medicare plan options. All the stuff the companies don't tell you. He is AMAZING!"

---Marilyn Koren (Williamsville, NY)

His Guidance Was Impeccable And Stress-Free

"I recently retired and was at my wits end receiving several different insurance companies quotes all costing me hundreds of "out-of-pocket" costs besides the upfront Medicare costs I have to pay. Andrew was so amazing to work with. He helped me make sense of it all in as little as 45 minutes. His guidance was impeccable and stress-free. They even reviewed all the new options for next year with me so I would know how to plan ahead. I have already given their name out to several of my friends. I "highly recommend" this service. Thank you again! You're so amazing at your profession!"

---Peg Mason (Alden, NY)

Save Yourself Countless Hours Spinning Your Wheels

"Andrew is simply the best possible choice you can make when getting ready to sign up and start Medicare. It gives me great piece of mind knowing he and his wife are around all year round for any follow up help I may need. Believe me you will be blown away by their extensive knowledge, professionalism, and superior service. You will never need to go anywhere else. Save yourself countless hours spinning your wheels at other places when this is the place you want to be!"

---June Brown (Depew, NY)

Worked Hard To Alleviate All My Anxiety

"Wonderful service. Andrew and his team are very knowledgeable, professional and patient! I was pretty anxious about turning 65 and needing Medicare. Calling Medicare directly had been less than helpful, but Andrew held my hand and worked hard to alleviate all my anxiety. I would recommend them very highly to anyone getting started with Medicare. They make the Medicare process very seamless and stress-free."

---Cynthia Marshall (Williamsville, NY)

Explained The Many Steps In
Easy To Understand Terms

"Andrew was so helpful in helping me with the Medicare process. He explained the many steps I needed to take to sign up in easy-to-understand terms --- and then offered to do it all for me --- for free! Gave me wonderful choices on companies that ended up saving me thousands of dollars compared to what I was thinking about doing. They are truly a gift I have received. I highly recommend anyone to explore their services before starting Medicare."

---John Duggan (Cheektowaga, NY)

They Took All The Confusion And Worry
Out Of The Process

"Medicare Management of WNY is AWESOME! Andrew educated me regarding all aspects of signing up for Medicare and choosing a private insurance plan that met my needs and my lifestyle. They took all the confusion and worry out of the process. I'm telling everyone I know about them, and several family members have already met with them. Don't hesitate! Schedule your session with Andrew when it's your turn to sign up for Medicare."

---Bob & Carol Mullins (Springville, NY)

Could Not Have Made The Whole Process
Any Easier Or Less Painful

"After so much time and frustration trying to walk through the Medicare Minefield on my own, Andrew could not have made the whole process any easier or less painful to get all my paperwork filled out and filed the right way without me having to do anything. Loved supporting this family-owned small business! Highly Recommend!

---John & Linda O'Connor (Ransomville, NY)

Saved Me So Much Time And Energy

"You guys saved me so much time and evenegy from having to figure all this out on me own! I will definitely be referring friends and family your way!"

---Paul & Joyce Wozniak (Depew, NY)

Had A Wonderful Experience
Working With Andrew

"Had a wonderful experience working with Andrew and Lyndsey. They were very knowledgable and patient. So glad we were referred to them when we were turning 65 and applying for Medicare."

---Joe & Darlene Fabozzi (Alden, NY)

I Walked Out Feeling Informed And Confident

"The time I spent with Andrew was EXCELLENT! He was very friendly and answered all my questions about if I need to sign up for Medicare if I'm still working or if I will be penalized if I wait to sign up. I was so nervous about Medicare, but he put me at ease with his knowledge. I walked our feeling informed and confident."

---Karen Bloom (East Aurora, NY)

We HIGHLY Recommend Medicare Management of WNY

"Our previous health insurance was always handled by one of our employers. When age 65 was nearing and we had to choose our own Medicare insurance, we were inundated and overwhelmed with mail, phone calls, and so-called "advice." At our meeting with (the very pleasant) Andrew, we finally understood Medicare. He is very knowledgeable, went over all aspects of what we needed to do, and could answer all the questions we asked (no matter how simple or complex they were). Before our meeting we felt we had no idea where to start. Leaving his office, we had step-by-step plan in place. We HIGHLY recommend Medicare Management of WNY and their SmartStart Program."

---Dan & Mary Gemmer (N. Tonawanda, NY)

Made The Medicare Process Easy And Understandable

"As my 65th birthday approaches, I've been inundated with Medicare flyers from every conceivable insurance provider. None of which are impartial. The government website is pretty much useless. Then I got referred to Andrew. Fantastic! Totally impartial and explained in real terms how Medicare works and how it doesn't work, too. And I can call whenever I have a question. Customer service EXTRAORDINAIRE!"

---Pam Barciniak (Williamsville, NY)

Went Above And Beyond

"Excellent personal service. Went above and beyond to help set us signed up and started with Medicare."

---Joe & Ruth Cicatello (Cheektowaga, NY)

We Couldn't Have Done It Without Andrew

"Went with my husband to get him signed up with Medicare. We were very impressed with the knowledge Andrew has and the manner of setting us at ease. We couldn't have done it without Andrew."

---Scott & Cheryl Rollo (Akron, NY)

Andrew Had All The Answers

"Very professional and knowledgeable. Andrew has all the answers to our questions and more. We are not retired yet, but he will be the first one we call when we do retire."

---Charles & Lynn Kobee (Williamsville, NY)

We Are Pleased To Recommend Them To Others

"We were very pleased with their handling of out Medicare B application. They were thorough, responsive to questions, kept us updated on progress, successfully and timely completed the process. We are pleased to recommend them to others."

---Art & Roberta Cagney (Kenmore, NY)

Clearly, I Have Been Misinformed By The Companies All This Time

"What an amazing afternoon...I met with Andrew about my Medicare coverage. He educated me about all the different companies and plans available to me. Clearly, I have been misinformed by the companies all this time before my meeting with Andrew. Feeling armed with the appropriate knowledge, he guided me through the whole process. I am so grateful."

---Paula Kuerzdoerfer (Springville, NY)

$4.00 FROM EVERY BOOK
DONATED TO SUPPORT

WNYHer es, **Inc.**
Supporting Western New York Veterans

Since inception in 2007, WNY Heroes, Inc. has grown exponentially, becoming a critical life sustaining vehicle for veterans and their families. Now, more than ever, a constant and critical need is growing in alarming fashion with so many veterans returning home and in need.

The mission of WNY Heroes, Inc is to provide veterans, their families, and the surviving spouses and children of veterans with financial assistance and resources that support their lives and sustain their dignity. This mission will be accomplished in two (2) ways:

- Provide monetary assistance to alleviate post-combat financial challenges, and…
- Provide positive support with health and housing needs, while also offering family care services through simple, yet essential gestures, such as delivering food, holiday gifts, and school supplies.

Medicare Management of WNY is proud to be a

153

supporting partner of WNY Heroes, Inc providing important and impactful financial funds to help sustain their ongoing efforts and stimulate expedited expansion.

In the future, a vision of creating and crafting a centralized resource will revolutionize the demand to meet, and exceed, the varying needs of veterans and their families in WNY through collaborations with community organizations.

HOW YOU CAN HELP

When you gift or give away copies of this book, *Starting Medicare Smartly,* to your friends and family and introduce them to our free Medicare SmartStart Program, $4.00 will be directly donated to support WNY Heroes, Inc through our ongoing "10-4 Impact Initiative."

- **Step 1** – Think of anyone you know who is turning 65 or getting ready to retire in the next 6-12 months?
- **Step 2** – Give them a copy of this book, share how our services helped you, and refer them to call us
- **Step 3** – In appreciation for your referral, we will send you $10.00, and donate $4.00 directly to WNY Heroes

A true WIN-WIN-WIN strategy. Your friends and family get the Medicare help they need. You get rewarded for your referrals. Veterans across WNY get the financial help they need. See "A Small Request" on how you can do your part.

A SMALL REQUEST

Thank you for reading *Starting Medicare Smartly*! I believe this book has the potential to help hundreds more in WNY, but to do that, I need your help.

Trust is rarely rational, but it is transferable. And in today's understandably untrusting world, I have to overcome the skepticism and suspicion surrounding anything mentioning Medicare, since folks are fearful of scams and swindlers.

I hope this book, and your introduction to me, broke down and disarmed your guarded gates, proving there are still good people, doing good things, for good reasons, just down the street you *can* still trust.

If you believe that to be true, would you be willing to share this book with the 3 people you know nearing age 65, or getting ready to retire, in the next 6-12 months? **We are on a mission dedicated to help 2,500 Baby Boomers in Buffalo sign up and start Medicare smartly by December 2025.**

You can call me at 716-833-0252 and I will send you free copies, at my expense, in exchange for your help doing your part to pay it forward. **Please, don't keep this book a secret!**

THE BETTER, SMARTER WAY TO SIGN UP FOR MEDICARE IN WNY YOU'VE NEVER HEARD OF!

Most folks in WNY aren't sure where to start with Medicare. And feeling forced to figure out all the fine print with what you have to do on your own is no place to be.

I have a proven, sure-fire solution for those who don't have the time or desire to deal with Medicare directly that makes the entire process, step-by-step from start to finish, simpler, easier, seemingly stress-free and almost effortless.

If you'd like to learn more about why my free Medicare SmartStart Program has quickly become the most popular and preferred way to sign up and start Medicare in WNY, and how it can be put to work for you, please request your FREE **"Medicare SmartStarter Info Kit"** today.

GET YOUR FREE INFO KIT HERE:

MedicareSmartStartWNY.com/Info

Or Call **716-833-0252** Or Scan

No Cost - No Risk - No Annoying Salesperson Will Answer

Made in the USA
Middletown, DE
19 June 2023

32777256R00088